WEIMAR AND NAZI GERMANY
c1918–1939

PETE JACKSON

The Publishers would like to thank the following for permission to reproduce copyright material.

Photo credits

p.10 © Everett Collection/Shutterstock; **p.13** © Sueddeutsche Zeitung Photo/Alamy Stock Photo; **p.14** © Art Media Factory – stock.adobe.com; **p.18** © Everett Collection/Shutterstock; **p.20** © Sueddeutsche Zeitung Photo/Alamy Stock Photo; **p.21** *t* © Bettman/Getty Images, *b* © Glasshouse Images/Alamy Stock Photo; **p.22** © Oleg_Mit/Shutterstock; **p.24** © Everett Collection/Shutterstock; **p.30** © Sueddeutsche Zeitung Photo/Alamy Stock Photo; **p.33** © Sueddeutsche Zeitung Photo/Alamy Stock Photo; **p.34** © Estate of George Grosz, Princeton, N.J./DACS 2024, Peter Barritt/Alamy Stock Photo; **p.38** © Everett Collection/Shutterstock; **p.40** © akg-images; **p.46** © Karl Schoendorfer/Shutterstock; **p.47** © World History Archive/Alamy Stock Photo; **p.51** © Chronicle/Alamy Stock Photo; **p.52** © Maurice Savage/Alamy Stock Photo; **p.53** © Shawshots / Alamy Stock Photo; **p.54** © INTERFOTO/Alamy Stock Photo; **p.55** © Look and Learn/Bridgeman Images; **p.56** © Sueddeutsche Zeitung Photo/Alamy Stock Photo; **p.57** © James E. Abbe/ullstein bild via Getty Images; **p.63** © Everett Collection/Shutterstock; **p.66** © World History Archive/Alamy Stock Photo; **p.71** © Everett/Shutterstock; **p.72** *t* © World History Archive/Alamy Stock Photo, *b* © ItzaVU/Shutterstock; **p.73** © Universal History Archive/Getty Images; **p.74** *t* © Kobal/Shutterstock, *b* © ARCHIVIO GBB/Alamy Stock Photo; **p.75** © David Cole/Alamy Stock Photo; **p.76** *t* © Pete Jackson, *b* © The Print Collector/Alamy Stock Photo; **p.77** © AF Fotografie/Alamy Stock Photo; **p.79** *t* © Sueddeutsche Zeitung Photo/Alamy Stock Photo, *b* © CBW/Alamy Stock Photo; **p.82** © Sueddeutsche Zeitung Photo/Alamy Stock Photo; **p.84** © neftali/Shutterstock; **p.87** © World History Archive/Alamy Stock Photo; **p.92** © Chronicle/Alamy Stock Photo; **p.96** © Artexplorer/Alamy Stock Photo; **p.97** © INTERFOTO/Alamy Stock Photo; **p.98** © Everett Collection/Shutterstock; **p.99** © Everett Collection Inc / Alamy Stock Photo; **p.101** © Shawshots/Alamy Stock Photo; **p.104** © Sueddeutsche Zeitung Photo/Alamy Stock Photo; **p.106** © Sueddeutsche Zeitung Photo/Alamy Stock Photo; **p.107** © Shawshots/Alamy Stock Photo; **p.110** © Photo 12/Alamy Stock Photo; **p.111** © GRANGER – Historical Picture Archive/Alamy Stock Photo; **p.113** © KGPA Ltd/Alamy Stock Photo; **p.114** © World History Archive/Alamy Stock Photo.

Although every effort has been made to ensure that website addresses are correct at time of going to press, Hodder Education cannot be held responsible for the content of any website mentioned in this book. It is sometimes possible to find a relocated web page by typing in the address of the home page for a website in the URL window of your browser.

Hachette UK's policy is to use papers that are natural, renewable and recyclable products and made from wood grown in well-managed forests and other controlled sources. The logging and manufacturing processes are expected to conform to the environmental regulations of the country of origin.

To order, please visit www.hoddereducation.com or contact Customer Service at education@hachette.co.uk / +44 (0)1235 827827.

ISBN: 978 1 3983 8935 9

© Peter Jackson 2024

First published in 2024 by
Hodder Education,
An Hachette UK Company
Carmelite House
50 Victoria Embankment
London EC4Y 0DZ

www.hoddereducation.com

The authorised representative in the EEA is Hachette Ireland, 8 Castlecourt Centre, Castleknock Road, Castleknock, Dublin 15, D15 YF6A, Ireland

Impression number   10 9 8 7 6 5 4 3 2 1

Year   2027 2026 2025 2024

All rights reserved. Apart from any use permitted under UK copyright law, no part of this publication may be reproduced or transmitted in any form or by any means, electronic or mechanical, including photocopying and recording, or held within any information storage and retrieval system, without permission in writing from the publisher or under licence from the Copyright Licensing Agency Limited. Further details of such licences (for reprographic reproduction) may be obtained from the Copyright Licensing Agency Limited, www.cla.co.uk

Cover photo © PictureLux / The Hollywood Archive / Alamy Stock Photo

Illustrations by Oxford Design & Illustrators, D'AVILA Illustration Agency and Aptara

Typeset in India

Printed and bound in Great Britain by Bell & Bain Ltd, Glasgow

A catalogue record for this title is available from the British Library.

CONTENTS

Introduction to the modern depth study — 4

Part 1: The Weimar Republic, 1918–29 — 10
1 The origins of the Republic, 1918–19 — 10
2 The early challenges to the Weimar Republic, 1919–23 — 16
3 The 'Golden Years': the recovery of the Republic, 1924–29 — 24
4 Changes in society, 1924–29 — 30

Part 2: Hitler's rise to power, 1919–33 — 38
1 Early development of the Nazi Party, 1920–22 — 38
2 The Munich Putsch and the Nazi Party, 1923–28 — 42
3 The growth in support for the Nazis, 1929–32 — 50
4 How Hitler became Chancellor, 1932–33 — 57

Part 3: Nazi control and dictatorship, 1933–39 — 63
1 The creation of a dictatorship, 1933–34 — 63
2 The police state — 71
3 Controlling and influencing attitudes — 74
4 Opposition, resistance and conformity — 83

Part 4: Life in Nazi Germany, 1933–39 — 91
1 Nazi policies towards women — 91
2 Nazi policies towards the young — 97
3 Employment and living standards — 103
4 The persecution of minorities — 109

Key words, individuals and events — 117
Index — 119

Introduction to the modern depth study

0.1 Your exam: What is assessed and how

The GCSE course that you are following is made up of four different studies.

	Paper 1: Thematic study and historic environment	Paper 2: Period study and British depth study	Paper 3: Modern depth study
What is assessed?	**Section A: Historic environment** This focuses on the relationship between a place and historical events and developments. **Section B: Thematic study** This focuses on change and continuity across a long sweep of history – from the medieval period to present day.	**Option P: Period study** This focuses on a wider world topic over a period of at least 50 years. **Option B: British depth study** This focuses on a period of British history over a short period of time (under 40 years).	This focuses on the complexity of a historical society or situation. The interplay of different aspects of history are considered.
How is it assessed?	Written exam: 1 hour 15 minutes 30% of your GCSE (52 marks) Section A – 3 compulsory questions (16 marks) Section B – 2 compulsory questions and 1 from a choice of 2 (36 marks)	Written exam: 1 hour 45 minutes 40% of your GCSE (64 marks) **Period study** – 2 compulsory questions and 2 from a choice of 3 (32 marks) **British depth study** – 2 compulsory questions and 1 from a choice of 2 (32 marks)	Written exam: 1 hour and 20 minutes 30% of your GCSE (52 marks) Section A – 2 compulsory questions (16 marks) Section B – 4 compulsory questions (36 marks)

This book prepares you for Paper 3 Modern depth study: Weimar and Nazi Germany, 1918–39.

It focuses on key developments in Germany between 1918 and 1939. This was a time period of dramatic change. You will study:

Part	Key content (topics)	Review pages
Part 1: The Weimar Republic, 1918–29	• The origins of the Republic, 1918–19 • The early challenges to the Weimar Republic, 1919–23 • The 'Golden Years': the recovery of the Republic, 1924–29 • Changes in society, 1924–29	Pages 36–37
Part 2: Hitler's rise to power, 1919–33	• Early development of the Nazi Party, 1920–22 • The Munich Putsch and the Nazi Party, 1923–28 • The growth in support for the Nazis, 1929–32 • How Hitler became Chancellor, 1932–33	Pages 61–62
Part 3: Nazi control and dictatorship, 1933–39	• The creation of a dictatorship, 1933–34 • The police state • Controlling and influencing attitudes • Opposition, resistance and conformity	Pages 89–90
Part 4: Life in Nazi Germany, 1933–39	• Nazi policies towards women • Nazi policies towards the young • Employment and living standards • The persecution of minorities	Pages 115–116

How the modern depth study will be examined

You will be examined on your knowledge and understanding of the modern depth study in Paper 3. The exam will be 1 hour 30 minutes. The table below gives you some guidance on writing time. You will need around 10 minutes or so to read the sources and interpretations for Question 3.

The table below shows the type of questions you will be asked. You should always spend up to a couple of minutes making sure you identify the focus of the question and planning your approach before you start to write your answer. This book will give you step-by-step guidance on how to tackle each type of question.

> **Revision Tip**
>
> **Break down your revision into manageable chunks of content**
>
> This book is organised into four parts that reflect the parts of the specification. At the end of each part of the course, make sure you review and revise what you have just covered. The 'Exam Practice', 'Recall Challenge' and 'Review' features will help you do this.

	Type of question	Guidance	Marks	Writing time	Advice and practice
1	Give two things you can infer from Source A about …	Focus on the question. Make an inference and then support with a quotation or detail from the source. Repeat for the second inference.	4	6 minutes	Pages 12, 15, 25, 31, 40, 45, 51, 54, 60, 76, 80
2	Explain why …	You will have a choice of two questions. Focus on the question and explain why an event or situation happened. Aim to write three paragraphs. Support your answer with at least three aspects of knowledge.	12	18 minutes	Pages 37, 49, 62, 70, 90, 104, 115
3a	How useful are Sources B and C for an enquiry into …	The sources could be visual or written. They will relate to an aspect of the enquiry in the question. Focus on how the sources are useful. Use the content of the source, the provenance of the source and your contextual knowledge to evaluate the usefulness of the sources.	8	12 minutes	Pages 28, 29, 41, 56, 68, 77, 82, 88, 96
3b	Study Interpretations 1 and 2. They give different views about … What is the main difference between these views?	Summarise the view in Interpretation 1 and support with a quotation. Summarise the view in Interpretation 2 and support with a quotation. Use the connective 'however' to summarise the overall difference between the two views.	4	6 minutes	Pages 28, 29, 45, 56, 88, 102, 108
3c	Suggest one reason why Interpretations 1 and 2 give different views about …	Explain that Interpretations 1 and 2 are different because: The authors have used different sources to form their view. The authors have chosen to focus on different aspects of the history. The authors have chosen to emphasis different aspects of the history.	4	6 minutes	Pages 28, 29, 45, 56, 88, 102, 108

Type of question		Guidance	Marks	Writing time	Advice and practice
3d	How far do you agree with Interpretation 2 about …	This is an essay question, requiring you to reach a judgement. Aim to agree with the view in Interpretation 2 using your own historical knowledge and then disagree with the view in Interpretation 2 using the view in Interpretation 1 and your own historical knowledge. Make sure that you write a conclusion explaining how far you agree with the view in Interpretation 2.	20 (16 + 4 for SPaG)	30 minutes	Pages 23, 28, 29, 56, 88, 102, 108

Revision Tips

Make exam practice part of your revision

Exam Tips give you step-by-step guidance on how to tackle each type of question. Effective revision is not just learning the content. You need to understand what each type of question is asking you to think about in the exam and to practise delivering it.

Take responsibility

Reflect on your strengths and weaknesses. What question types do you struggle with? Take responsibility: spend more time practising the types of question you find most difficult. Use feedback from your teacher to improve your approach.

0.2 The big picture: Identify the big questions

Connect & Engage

The following topic summaries identify the people and big questions the book will cover. However, top historians do not answer only other people's questions, they also ask tions of their own! As you read the summary of each topic, note down any questions you might have about this topic.

Part 1: The Weimar Republic, 1918–29			
Topic 1: The origins of the Republic, 1918–19	**Topic 2: The early challenges to the Weimar Republic, 1919–23**	**Topic 3: The 'Golden Years': the recovery of the Republic, 1924–29**	**Topic 4: Changes in society, 1924–29**
The Weimar Republic was a new democratic government created after the abdication of Kaiser Wilhelm II in 1918. Its constitution made it one of the most democratic countries in the world.	The Weimar Republic faced challenges including the Treaty of Versailles. It faced the Spartacist Rising, led in part by Rosa Luxemburg, and an economic crisis called hyperinflation in 1923.	In these years, the Weimar Republic enjoyed a period of political stability and economic recovery, in which politician Gustav Stresemann was instrumental. Loans from the USA enabled the German economy to grow.	German society changed hugely. Culture was vibrant and Germany became the centre of the film industry.

Part 2: Hitler's rise to power, 1919–33

Topic 5: Early development of the Nazi Party, 1920–22	Topic 6: The Munich Putsch and the Nazi Party, 1923–28	Topic 7: The growth in support for the Nazis, 1929–32	Topic 8: How Hitler became Chancellor, 1932–33
Adolf Hitler joined the Nazi Party and transformed it. He set out the party's goals in the 25-point programme.	The Nazi Party tried to take power by force in the Munich Putsch of November 1923. It failed and Hitler was imprisoned. The Nazi Party only gained 12 seats in the May 1928 election.	In the early 1930s, support for the Nazis grew dramatically. This was due to an economic crisis sparked by the Wall Street Crash of 1929.	Hitler was appointed Chancellor of Germany in January 1933 by President Paul von Hindenburg. This was because the Nazis had the most support in Germany but also due to politicians such as Franz von Papen.

Part 3: Nazi control and dictatorship, 1933–39

Topic 9: The creation of a dictatorship, 1933–34	Topic 10: The police state	Topic 11: Controlling and influencing attitudes	Topic 12: Opposition, resistance and conformity
As Chancellor, Hitler set about getting rid of democracy. Events like the Reichstag Fire, Enabling Act and Night of the Long Knives helped him increase his powers. When President von Hindenburg died in August 1934, Hitler became Führer.	The Nazis controlled the German people using the SS under the leadership of Heinrich Himmler. The law courts were taken over by the Nazis and the Nazis aimed to control the Church.	The Nazis used propaganda to control people. Joseph Goebbels was in charge of censorship and propaganda.	There was opposition to the Nazis mostly from the Churches and young people. Pastor Martin Niemöller was a key opponent.

Part 4: Life in Nazi Germany, 1933–39

Topic 13: Nazi policies towards women	Topic 14: Nazi policies towards the young	Topic 15: Employment and living standards	Topic 16: The persecution of minorities
The Nazis wanted a traditional way of life for German women. They wanted women to be mothers and made it more difficult for women to have jobs or go to university.	Hitler said 'Those who have youth on their side control the future'. Hitler created Nazi youth groups and used education to indoctrinate young people into supporting Nazi ideals.	The Nazis promised people 'work and bread' and by 1939 had largely reduced unemployment in Germany. They created organisations such as Beauty of Labour and Strength Through Joy to influence living standards.	The Nazis targeted minority groups such as Jewish people, black people, LGBTQ+ people, disabled people and Roma and Sinti communities. 'Kristallnacht' in 1938 (Night of the Broken Glass) was a key turning point in the treatment of Jewish people.

0.3 Key features: How this book works

The tasks in this book will help you learn what you need to know and how to apply your knowledge to answer exam questions effectively. They are your **'steps to success'**.

Research & Record

This gets your learning into your head in the first place and into your notebooks. It will start you thinking in a way that will help you produce good answers to the exam questions.

Each **research question** reflects an issue that examiners will expect you to be an expert on. Complete these tasks, which build an answer to each research question, carefully and neatly because they will become your revision notes. Many tasks use tables. Give yourself room – each table should have its own page in your books.

> If you have gaps in your knowledge, go back to your research notes and the relevant section of this book and make sure that you add anything that is missing so you have covered all the key topics in enough detail.

Summarise

This turns your learning into a **memorable form**. Sometimes we guide you to do this, but mostly it is up to you.

Memory aids are different from your research notes. They use images or diagrams but few words. Most people remember better if something is summarised with both text and visuals.

> If you cannot remember some of the content you have covered, go back to your research notes and improve or recreate your memory aid.

Connect & Engage

These tasks make you form **connections** between what you have already learned and what you are about to learn.

Apply ▶ Recall Challenge

Prepare yourself for exams by testing yourself on what you have learned.

Quizzes, games and competitions test how much you can remember. They identify your weak spots where you need to spend more time.

Apply ▶ Exam Practice

Continue to prepare for the exam by answering exam-style questions with our Exam Tips to guide you.

Our **practice questions** are like the questions you will be asked in the exam, although none come from actual past papers. You can get real papers from your teacher or the EdExcel website. There are **Exam Tips** for each question type so you know how to approach it.

> If you did not understand how to approach an exam question, go back to the Exam Tips in this book and re-read them, checking that you fully understand what is required in a good answer to that type of question.

Review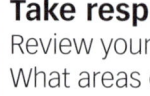

We regularly **review** the **big ideas and concepts**. We also encourage you to **review your own learning**.

> **Take responsibility**
> Review your own learning. What areas did you do well on? What areas do you need to improve?

Revision Tips

1. **Don't delay** revision until just before the exam
   Revision should be an ongoing process. You need to revisit topics that you have studied regularly. Otherwise, as the graph shows, you will quickly start to forget key topics.
2. **Retrieval practice** makes your memory stronger
   When you recall what you have previously studied, your brain strengthens connections and makes it easier to recall this information in the future.
3. **Spaced practice** helps you remember for longer!
   At the end of each topic, we test you, not just on that topic but on previous ones as well. You should regularly return to the Review tasks from previous topics and test your knowledge of 'older material'. As the graph shows, this should improve recall and stop you forgetting.

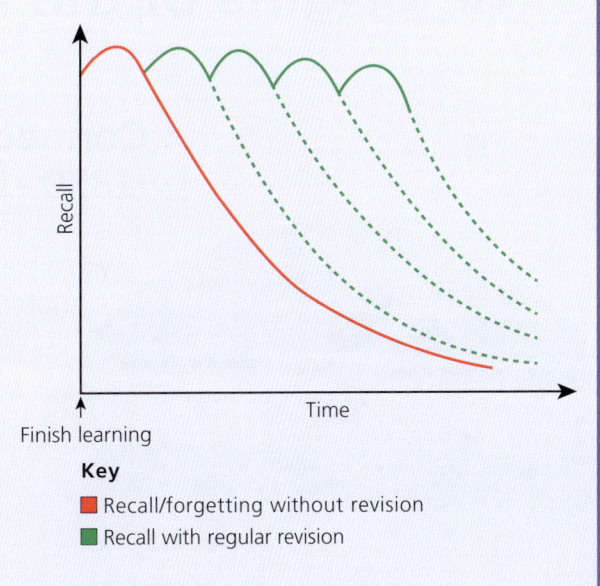

Key
- Recall/forgetting without revision
- Recall with regular revision

Apply ▶ Recall Challenge

Know your individuals

How much can you remember from the 'big picture' of the Germany course? Match each of the individuals to the correct description.

Individual	Description
Adolf Hitler	Leading Nazi who was in charge of propaganda
Gustav Stresemann	Leading Nazi who was in charge of the SS
Martin Niemöller	Leader of the Nazi Party who became Chancellor of Germany in January 1933
Paul von Hindenburg	Politician who helped Germany recover from its problems between 1924 and 1929
Rosa Luxemburg	President from 1925 to 1934 who appointed Hitler as Chancellor
Heinrich Himmler	One of the leaders of the Spartacist Rising of 1919
Joseph Goebbels	Church leader and opponent of the Nazis

Know your key dates

Match each event to the year it happened.

Year	Event
1918	The Spartacist Rising
1919	Wall Street Crash
1923	'Kristallnacht' (Night of the Broken Glass)
1929	Abdication of Kaiser Wilhelm II leads to Weimar Republic
1933	Death of President von Hindenburg
1934	Hyperinflation crisis
1938	Adolf Hitler becomes Chancellor of Germany

1 The origins of the Republic, 1918–19

Connect & Engage – Kaiser Wilhelm II (1859–1941)

Kaiser Wilhelm II ruled Germany from 1888 to 1918. He was born with a partly paralysed left arm that was said to be six inches shorter than his right arm. Due to this, he had a difficult childhood and often felt he had to prove himself.

Wilhelm was related to royal families across Europe, including Britain, Norway, Spain, Greece and Russia. He was the eldest grandson of Queen Victoria. He visited England regularly and came to admire Britain's navy and the British Empire.

Kaiser Wilhelm II was known for his explosive temper and being indecisive. He was also highly intelligent and his interest in science and technology led to him setting up an institution to advance scientific research in 1911.

Wilhelm's policies and beliefs

Wilhelm became Kaiser at the age of just 29 and he said himself he was not ready to be Emperor. However, he set about modernising Germany. He wanted Germany to become a powerful military country and have its own empire. He called this policy **Weltpolitik** (world politics). He oversaw the expansion of Germany's navy. Wilhelm was against democracy and believed that the Kaiser should be an autocratic ruler. This meant only he could make decisions. He was furious when the words 'Dem Deutschen Volke' which means 'To the German people' were put onto the **Reichstag** (German Parliament) building in 1916.

In August 1914, Kaiser Wilhelm led Germany into the First World War. The war quickly became a long, drawn-out conflict. As the war continued, people in Germany faced economic and social hardship. The impact of this and military defeats led to protests in Germany. On 9 November 1918, the **German Revolution** led to Kaiser Wilhelm **abdicating** (giving up) his position as Kaiser. His rule was at an end. Wilhelm went into exile in the Netherlands where he lived until his death in June 1941 at the age of 82.

Connect & Engage

1. Read the story of Kaiser Wilhelm II above. What impression do you get of the kind of ruler he was?
2. Check your understanding of these key words in the text: Weltpolitik, autocratic, Reichstag, abdicate, Kaiser.

1.1 The impact of the First World War on Germany

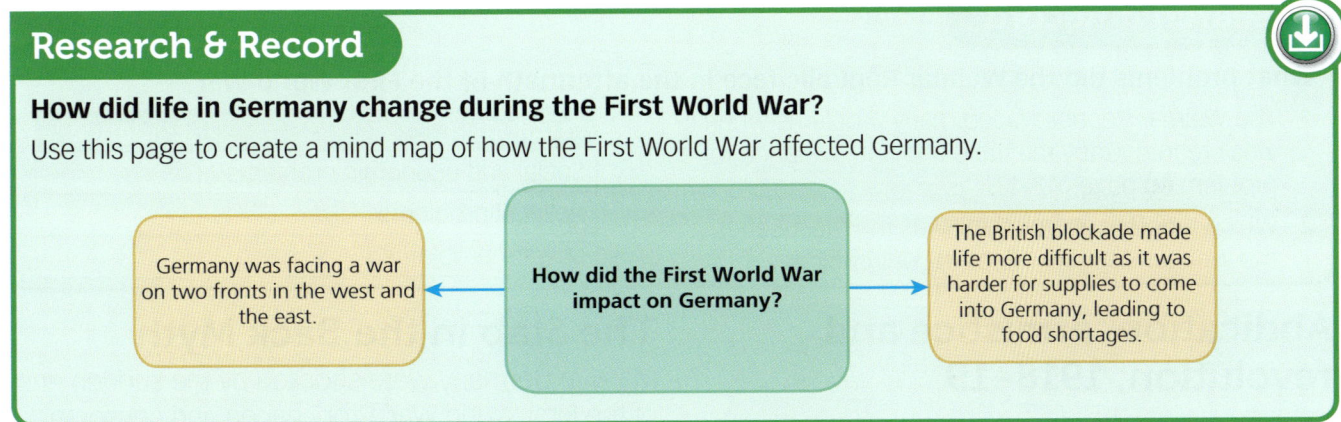

The events of the First World War

The First World War broke out in August 1914. Germany fought alongside Austria-Hungary, Bulgaria and Turkey. Germany fought the First World War on two fronts. It fought against Britain and France in the west and against Russia in the east. The USA joined the war on the side of Britain and France in April 1917 – Britain, France, Russia and the USA were known as the Allies.

Germany had some early successes, such as at the Battle of Tannenberg against the Russians in August 1914. However, the war quickly developed into a stalemate on the Western Front with neither side able to achieve a breakthrough. Despite this, the German public were led to believe through **propaganda** that the war was going well for Germany. Russia left the war in March 1918 after the Bolshevik Revolution of October 1917. This led to. Germany launching a huge attack in the west called the Spring Offensive. The attack was a partial success. In some places, the German army advanced up to 40 miles. However, the Allies counter-attacked in August 1918 and by September it was clear that Germany had been defeated.

Life in Germany during the war

There was no actual fighting in Germany during the First World War but life changed dramatically for ordinary people. During the war, the British Navy placed a blockade of ships around the North German coast. This prevented supplies and resources getting to Germany. There were shortages and many German people only had basic foods like turnips to eat. People in Germany became war-weary as time went on, wages were low and many families had lost loved ones in the war. By 1918, there was an increase in strikes, protests and discontent within Germany.

1.2 The situation in Germany at the end of the War

Research & Record

What problems did the Weimar Republic face in the aftermath of the First World War?

1. The Weimar Republic faced many problems when it was created. Copy the table and find evidence for each problem on pages 12–13.
2. Which problem do you think was the most serious for the Weimar Republic? Explain your choice.

Problem	Evidence
Social and economic problems	
Political problems	
Military problems	

Abdication, armistice and revolution, 1918–19

The war quickly developed into a stalemate on the Western Front with neither side able to achieve a breakthrough. Protests and unrest spread across Germany including a mutiny of sailors at Kiel on 3 November. This led to the Kaiser abdicating on 9 November. A new government that would come to be known as the **Weimar Republic** was formed. On 11 November 1918, the **Chancellor** of the new German government, Friedrich Ebert, accepted an **armistice** with the Allies. Plans were made to hold elections to make Germany a democracy. These dramatic uprisings and political change were known as the German Revolution.

The Stab in the Back Myth

Many in Germany were shocked by the sudden end of the First World War. Propaganda and censorship had convinced most Germans they were winning the war. This meant that to many, defeat was unexpected. This led to the idea of the **Stab in the Back Myth** (Dolchstosslegende). This was the belief that Germany had not been properly defeated in the First World War but had been betrayed by weak politicians who took power after the Kaiser's abdication. These politicians became known as the November Criminals. This idea was false, but it created problems for the new German government. Nationalist politicians, such as Hitler, used the myth to attack the Weimar Republic.

▶ **Source A** Kaiser Wilhelm II writing about the 'Stab in the Back Myth' in his memoirs in 1922

> For thirty years, the army was my pride. For it I lived, upon it I laboured, and now, after four and a half brilliant years of war with unprecedented victories, it was forced to collapse by the stab in the back from the dagger of the revolutionist, at the very moment when peace was within reach.

Apply ▶ Exam Practice

Question 1 style

Give two things you can infer from Source A about Kaiser Wilhelm's view on Germany's defeat in the First World War. **(4 marks)**

What can you infer?	Evidence from the source to support this

Exam Tip

Making inferences from a source (Question 1)

You will be asked to make two inferences from a source. To do this successfully, you must look beyond what you can see or what is written in the source and think about what this information suggests. You are looking for what is not shown or said in the source. In your exam, it is important that you use **only the source**, not your own knowledge. For example, when answering this question:

- In the source you are told that the Kaiser refers to 'unprecedented victories in the war'.
- From this, one thing that we can infer is that the Kaiser did not believe the army was to blame for Germany losing the First World War.

Germany's problems

The legacy of the First World War was immense and left a challenging situation for Germany at the end of the war.

- Inflation was high in Germany. This meant the price of goods was increasing quickly. People could not afford goods because wages were not increasing.

- There was a huge increase in the number of strikes since the autumn of 1918. In 1919, around 34 million working days were lost to strikes.

- 1.5 million soldiers had to leave the military and return home. Many soldiers had been injured or wounded in the First World War and would need to be looked after.

- Ever since the winters of 1916 and 1917 there had been huge shortages of food and fuel in Germany. This caused hardship, especially in the cities, with thousands of people starving to death.

- German Communists had been inspired by the events of the Communist Revolution of 1917 in Russia. They wanted an armed revolution in Germany.

- The Allies kept the blockade of Germany's coastline even after the Armistice of November 1918. This led to further shortages. The blockade did not end until June 1919.

- There was a flu epidemic. The 'Spanish flu' killed as many as 260,000 people in Germany.

- There was a growing number of military-style groups, many of which were formed from ex-soldiers. These were called the **Freikorps**. They were all anti-communist. Many of them were right-wing and hostile to the new German government. They were angry about Germany's defeat in the First World War and believed in the Stab in the Back Myth – the idea Germany had not been properly defeated.

- The Armistice of 11 November 1918 was just an agreement to stop fighting. Germany still had to negotiate a peace treaty to end the First World War. Many in Germany were nervous about the effects of a peace treaty on Germany.

- It also had to come up with a **constitution**. A constitution is a system of rules which sets out how a country should be run.

- The situation in Berlin was very tense with violence and disorder. Fighting on the streets meant that the new German government had to move to the town of Weimar in central Germany in order to begin to solve Germany's problems.

▲ The mutiny of sailors at Kiel on 3 November 1918. This was an important event within the German Revolution.

1.3 The new Weimar Constitution

Research & Record

What were the strengths and weaknesses of the Weimar Constitution?

Use pages 14–15 to complete your own copy of a table like this. Record the strengths and weaknesses of the Weimar Constitution.

Strengths	Weaknesses

The first elections

The new Weimar government held elections for the German Parliament (Reichstag) in January 1919. The results in the table below show how many different political parties there were. Each party had different ideas on how to solve Germany's problems.

The Weimar Republic was called a Republic because it had no monarch. It was named after a town in central Germany called Weimar where the government was based between February and August 1919.

One of the first tasks was to make a constitution for the new government. A draft was made by February 1919 and the final constitution was completed and agreed in August 1919.

Political party	Number of seats in the Reichstag
Social Democratic Party (SPD)	165
German Democratic Part (DDP)	75
Centre Party (ZP)	91
German National People's Party (DNVP)	44
Independent Social Democratic Party of Germany (USPD)	22
Bavarian People's Party (BVP)	20
German People's Party (DVP)	19
Others	7

▲ Results of the January 1919 elections for the Reichstag

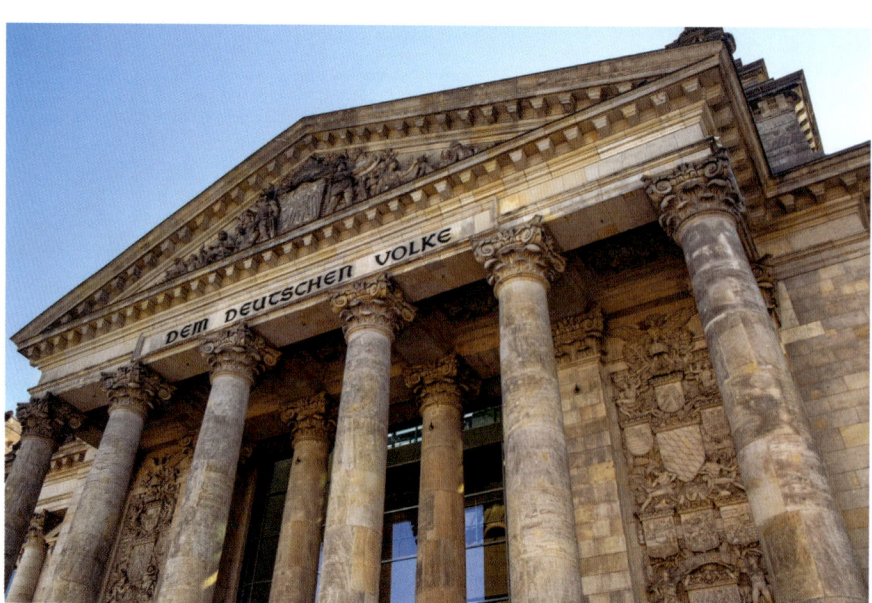

▶ The Reichstag is the German Parliament. The words 'Dem Deutschen Volke' mean 'To the German people'

The Weimar Constitution

The Weimar Constitution began a new era for Germany. Germany became one of the most democratic countries in the world. Men and women could both vote from the age of 20. All Germans had equal rights, free speech and freedom of religion. The head of the government was known as the Chancellor and had to have the support of the Reichstag (German Parliament). Voting was done by proportional representation. This is a voting system which means political parties get seats in a parliament directly according to how many votes they got. This was really fair. Under the Weimar Constitution, a political party that got 20 per cent of votes got roughly 20 per cent of seats in the Reichstag.

The Weimar Constitution was democratic and although there were some potential weaknesses, democracy in the early 1920s survived many different challenges from both Left and Right. Although the proportional representation system meant several parties had to work together, this generally worked well in the 1920s. However, this would cause problems in the early 1930s, when political parties could not agree on how to solve the severe economic problems of the Great Depression. In addition, the voting system meant enemies of Weimar democracy such as the Nazi Party got seats in the Reichstag. There were some people in Germany who would have preferred the rule of the Kaiser rather than a democracy. However, it is important to note that Weimar democracy did oversee a number of important political changes succesfully. For example, they reduced the size of the armed forces after the First World War and they provided money for unemployed people.

Article 48 of the Weimar Constitution gave the President the power to make laws in an emergency. This meant that a President could rule without the Reichstag's approval in an emergency situation. This would happen in the early 1930s when Germany was suffering from the political and economic effects of the Great Depression.

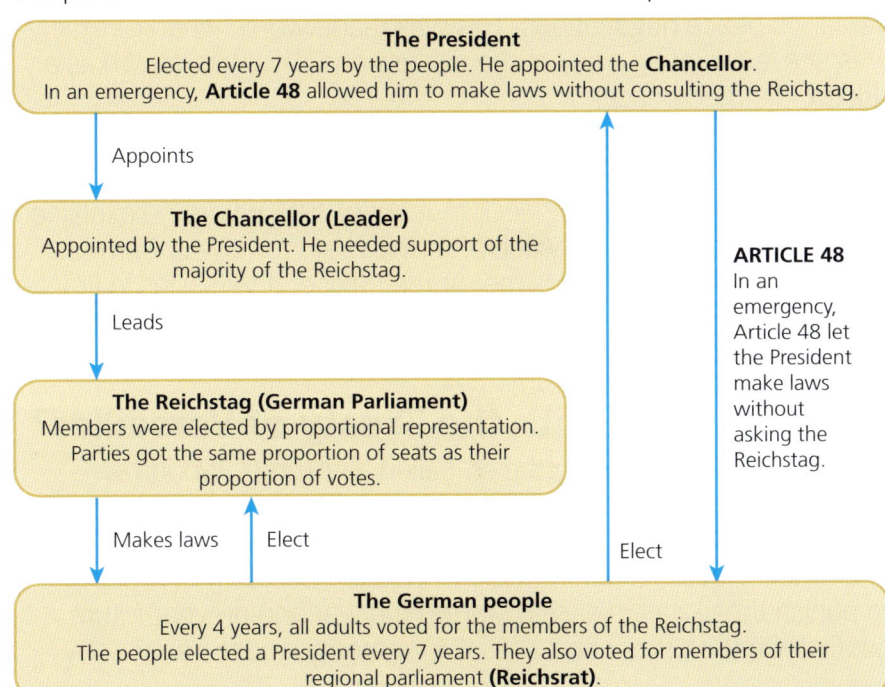

◀ Summary of the constitution of the Weimar Republic

▶ **Source B** From a speech of the new Constituent Assembly by Hugo Preuss, head of the Commission that drew up the Weimar Constitution in 1919. Here, he is talking about the new constitution.

I have often listened to the debates with real concern, glancing timidly to the gentlemen of the Right, fearful lest they say to me: 'Do you hope to give a parliamentary system to a nation like this, one that resists it with every sinew in its body?' One finds suspicion everywhere; Germans cannot shake off their old timidity and their deference to the authoritarian state.

Apply ▶ Exam Practice

Question 1 style

Give two things you can infer from Source B about the Weimar Constitution. (4 marks)

Exam Tip

Making inferences from a source (Question 1)

1. Some students struggle with how to start their answer. Start your answer by **using the key phrase in the question**. This should help you to focus on the question as well as to get started!
2. Do not simply describe the source. You need to **make an inference** from the source and **support** it with a detail that you can see or a quotation if it is a written source.

2 The early challenges to the Weimar Republic, 1919–23

2.1 Why did Germany dislike the Treaty of Versailles?

Research & Record

Why did Germany dislike the Treaty of Versailles?

Make your own copy of the table below. While you read pages 16–17, complete the second column to explain each reason why Germany disliked the Treaty of Versailles. When you have completed all reasons, evaluate the importance of each in column 3.

Reason	Explanation. How did it lead to Germany disliking the Treaty?	Evaluation. How important was it for making Germany dislike the Treaty?
Land		
Army		
Money		
Blame		
Dictated peace		
Wilson's 14 Points		

The Stab in the Back Myth

The Stab in the Back Myth (see page 12) meant many in Germany were already angry about the end of the First World War and the Versailles peace negotiations. This was made worse when Germany wasn't even allowed a say at the discussions. This was known as a **diktat** (dictated peace).

Wilson's 14 Points

Woodrow Wilson made a speech in January 1918 where he explained his 14 Points for bringing peace after the First World War. Germany thought that when the Allies met at the Palace of Versailles in France in June 1919, the peace treaty would be based on 'Wilson's 14 Points' which many believed would have been fairer towards Germany.

Who came up with the Treaty of Versailles?

The Treaty was decided by the so-called 'Big Three': Woodrow Wilson (President of the USA), David Lloyd-George (Prime Minister of Britain), and Georges Clemenceau (Prime Minister of France). France and Britain wanted a harsh treaty to weaken Germany in order to punish those they believed started the war and prevent future conflict. On the other hand, the USA wanted a kinder treaty. They

▶ **Source A** From a German newspaper, *Deutsche Zeitung*, 28 June

Vengeance! German nation! Today in the Hall of Mirrors [at Versailles] the disgraceful treaty is being signed. Do not forget it. The German people will, with unceasing work, press forward to reconquer the place among nations to which it is entitled. Then will come vengeance for the shame of 1919.

were worried about a weaker Germany falling to **communism**.

How did German people react?

The **Treaty of Versailles** was announced on 28 June 1919. Almost everyone in Germany was furious. They blamed politicians of the Weimar Republic for the peace treaty. Germany felt humiliated and this led to political unrest in the years that followed.

What were the terms of the Treaty of Versailles?

Loss of land

Germany lost 10 per cent of its land, which contained 13 per cent of its population. This included all its overseas colonies and land containing important raw materials including 26 per cent of its coal. The main changes are shown on the map below.

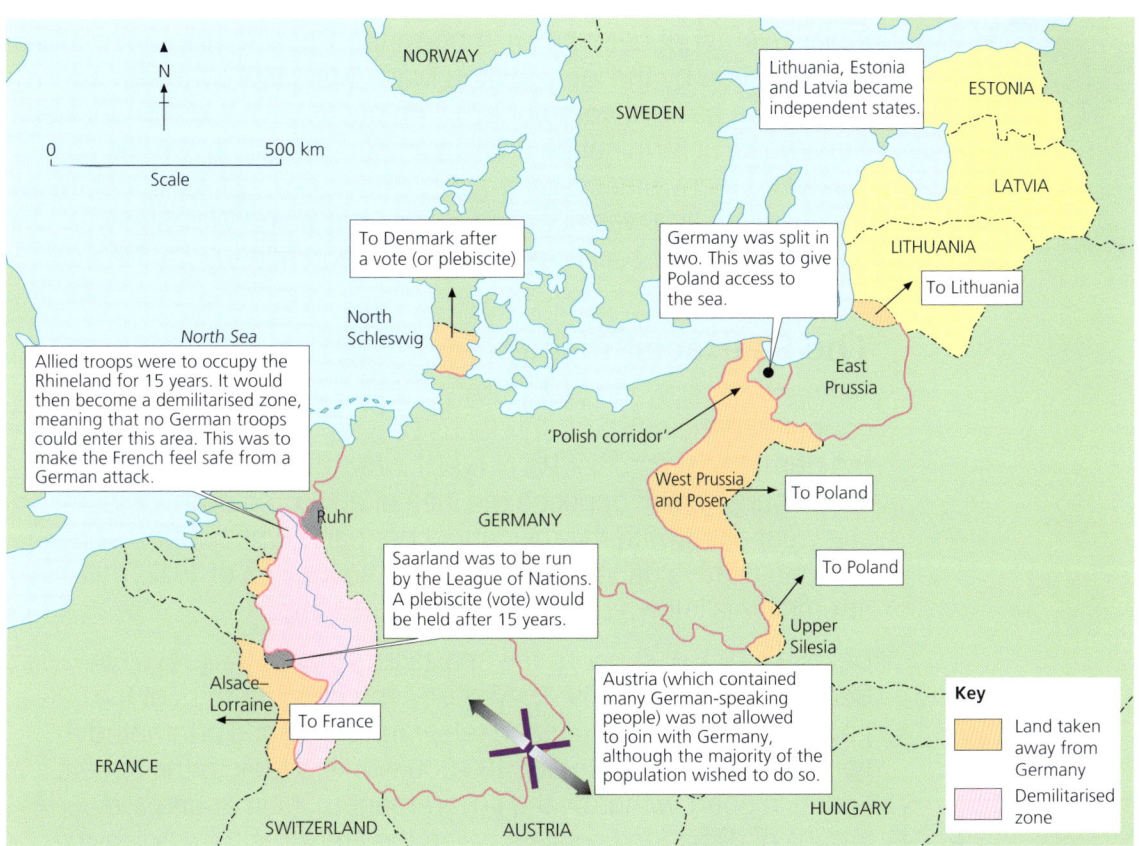

Armed forces

The size of the German army was seen as a threat to other countries in Europe, especially France. Major restrictions were placed on German armed forces:

- Germany was not allowed tanks, submarines or an air force.
- The navy could only build six battleships.
- The German army was reduced to 100,000 men.
- Conscription was banned (the government could not force Germans to join the army – they had to be volunteers).

Blame for the First World War

Article 231 of the Treaty of Versailles made Germany accept blame for starting the First World War which let the Allies demand compensation from Germany for the damage. Germans found this very unfair.

Reparations

Germany had to pay **reparations** (a fine) for the damage done in the First World War. Most of the money would go to France and Belgium. No final sum was fixed at Versailles. In 1921, the Allies fixed the final amount at £6,600 million. This was broken down into annual payments.

2.2 Challenges to the Weimar Republic

Connect & Engage – Rosa Luxemburg (1871–1919)

Rosa Luxemburg was born in Poland. As a disabled (she had a limp) Jewish woman, she was treated as a second-class citizen in Russian-occupied Poland. Even though society made her life harder than necessary, she gained a doctorate in political economy at the University of Zurich in Switzerland, and became Dr Rosa Luxemburg. At the time, not many women had achieved this.

Rosa Luxemburg became an important political thinker whose ideas were inspired by the ideas of Karl Marx (Marxism), whose theories formed the basis of communism. She became well known for her cleverness, determination and inspirational public speaking. She was jailed many times as she wrote and spoke against the dangers of capitalism and was opposed to the First World War. She was passionate about social justice, equality and fighting for the rights of the poor.

▲ Rosa Luxemburg, Spartacist leader

The Spartacist Rising

During the First World War, Rosa Luxemburg and Karl Liebknecht co-founded the anti-war Spartacus League, which would become the German Communist Party (KPD). After the German Revolution, Luxemburg herself opposed the idea of an armed uprising, but she went along with the majority of her party who supported a communist revolution, like the Russian Revolution of 1917. This attempt was known as the **Spartacist Rising**.

Despite a lack of support, the Spartacists began their revolt in Berlin on 5 January 1919. They seized the headquarters of the government's newspaper and telegraph office and attempted a general strike. On 6 January, 100,000 workers took to the streets. Friedrich Ebert withdrew the government to Weimar and allowed groups of disbanded soldiers called the Freikorps to restore order.

The Freikorps drove the Spartacists off the streets by mid-January. On 15 January, Rosa Luxemburg and Karl Liebknecht were both arrested and murdered by the Freikorps. Luxemburg was beaten up, shot and her body was dumped in a canal.

Even today, each January people march in memory of Rosa Luxemburg. Her ideas have stood the test of time and still inspire many people to fight for justice and a better world.

▶ **Source B** Rosa Luxemburg

I want to burden the conscience of the affluent with all the suffering and all the hidden, bitter tears.

Connect & Engage

1. Read the story of Rosa Luxemburg. What kind of leader do you think she was?
2. Why do you think the story of Rosa Luxemburg still inspires people today?

Research & Record

Who opposed the Weimar Republic between 1919 and 1922?

Create a detailed mind map as you read pages 18–19 to show the different groups who were against the Weimar Republic between 1919 and 1922. Include the Spartacists, Freikorps, Kapp Putsch and political violence.

Supporters and opponents of the Weimar Republic

Political groups can be organised into left-wing, centre and right-wing. Political parties in the centre are sometimes called **moderate**. These parties mostly supported the Weimar Republic. The extremes opposed the Weimar Republic. The Spartacists were the extreme left-wing.

The Political Spectrum		
Extreme left-wing	**Parties supporting the Weimar Republic**	**Extreme right-wing**
The **Communist Party** believed in equality and sharing out wealth. They wanted the government to take control of private businesses and property. The Spartacists were German Communists.	**Social Democrats** – their leader, Ebert, was a key figure in the Weimar Republic and was elected President in 1919. **Centre Party** – represented Catholic Church. **Democratic Party** – mainly supported by the middle class. **People's Party** – support came from the middle class and factory owners. Its leader was **Gustav Stresemann**.	**German National Party** (DNVP) wanted Germany to have a strong leader like the Kaiser. They were against the Treaty of Versailles and wanted Germany to be militarily strong. The **Nazi Party** were a violent and nationalistic political party which had a racist and antisemitic world view.

The Kapp Putsch

Ebert had used the Freikorps to put down the Spartacist Rising. The Freikorps were groups of disbanded soldiers in Germany. Many Germans, including the Freikorps, hated the Treaty of Versailles and the Weimar Republic for signing it. The main problem was with the army. It hated the 100,000 limit placed on it and blamed the government for agreeing to it. The army was reduced in size to follow the Treaty, but many of the ex-soldiers simply joined the Freikorps.

By early 1920, the Allies were worried about the size of these unofficial armies. They put pressure on Germany to remove them. The government tried to do this in March 1920. This resulted in 12,000 Freikorps men attempting to march into Berlin and declare a new national government. They were led by Wolfgang Kapp, a Prussian civil servant and Walther von Lüttwitz. The army refused to stop the Freikorps. General Seeckt, a senior officer in the Defence Ministry, famously said that 'Troops do not fire on troops' and refused to defend the Weimar Republic.

The Weimar government was powerless. It fled to Dresden, and asked German workers to save it. The workers called a General Strike, cutting off gas, electricity, food and coal supplies. This led to the **Kapp Putsch** collapsing in just a few days and Kapp fled to Sweden. The people who took part in the putsch were never punished. General Seeckt was even promoted and became chief of the army command. The army would continue to act outside government authority and often went against the Treaty of Versailles.

Political violence

Political violence continued to affect the Weimar Republic after March 1920. Between 1919 and 1922 there were 376 political murders. 354 of these murders were carried out by right-wing groups. Political parties had their own private armies. These unoffical armies included a group called the Stalhelm (Steel Helmets) who were linked to the DNVP, and the **Sturmabteilung (SA)**, who were run by the Nazi Party. Important Weimar politicians were assassinated. The years 1919 to 1922 were filled with violence, disorder and chaos. However, it would be 1923 that became the year of crisis for the Weimar Republic.

2.3 The challenges of 1923

1923 was a year of crisis for the Weimar Republic. Problems with paying reparations led to the French occupying an industrial area of Germany known as the **Ruhr**. Inflation is when the prices of goods rise and this had been happening in Germany since the First World War. During 1923, inflation rose so dramatically that it was known as **hyperinflation**.

Research & Record

What were the causes and consequences of the hyperinflation crisis?

On your own copy of the 'bingo card', answer as many questions as you can using the information on the next three pages. Start by trying to get a complete row or column. Who can be the first to get a 'full house'?

Hyperinflation bingo		
1. Who invaded the Ruhr in 1923?	2. What caused hyperinflation in Germany?	3. Give an example of how Germans resisted the invasion of the Ruhr.
4. Who gained from hyperinflation?	5. Who lost from hyperinflation?	6. What does the story of Hugo Stinnes tell us about hyperinflation?
7. How did Gustav Stresemann help bring about the end of hyperinflation?	8. Why was 1923 such a crisis year for the Weimar Republic?	9. What do you predict might be the longer-term impact of the hyperinflation crisis on Germany?

The occupation of the Ruhr

In November 1922, Germany announced that they could no longer afford the reparations payments. This led to French and Belgian troops occupying the Ruhr, an industrial area within the western part of Germany. France and Belgium did not believe that Germany could not afford the reparations and therefore decided to take payment in goods from the Ruhr industrial area.

Passive resistance

German workers in the Ruhr reacted to the occupation with **passive resistance**. This meant that they refused to cooperate with French and Belgian soldiers and went on strike. At times, there was violence and some German workers used sabotage tactics such as breaking machines and equipment, setting factories on fire or flooding mines. The occupation created tension between Germany and France.

The consequences of the occupation

The occupation of the Ruhr helped to unite the German people behind the Weimar Republic against the aggression of France and Belgium. Some of the strikers were seen as heroes in terms of standing up to the Treaty of Versailles. As a result, the German government supported the strikers. This meant they had to pay them, but the government was running out of money. Consequently, it began to print more money to pay the striking workers. However, printing money in this way leads to inflation and when it is on a large scale, it leads to hyperinflation. This is because the more money that is available, the less it is worth.

▲ A French soldier in the Ruhr, 1923

How did hyperinflation affect the German people?

Hyperinflation is when the prices of goods rise very dramatically (see the table below).

Item for sale	1913	Summer 1923	November 1923
1 kg of bread	0.29	1,200	428,000,000,000 428 billion
1 kg of butter	2.70	26,000	6,000,000,000,000 6 trillion
1 kg of beef	1.75	18,800	5,600,000,000,000 5.6 trillion
1 pair of shoes	12.00	1,000,000	32,000,000,000,000 32 trillion

▲ Prices in the hyperinflation crisis (in German marks)

People across Germany were affected differently by hyperinflation. Some people gained while others lost out. The middle classes were particularly badly affected while the upper classes had resources such as land which kept their wealth.

Winners of hyperinflation	Losers of hyperinflation
Some business people, such as **Hugo Stinnes**, gained by buying companies using cheap loans.	People on fixed incomes such as people on pensions.
People with lots of debts could repay loans with worthless money.	Middle class professionals who were paid monthly – their income did not keep pace with inflation.
Shortages led to a rise in food prices which helped farmers.	Those with lots of savings found they had become worthless.
Some people had lots of foreign currency such as dollars, so were not affected, because foreign money kept its value.	Some farmers were reluctant to sell food for worthless money. This led to food shortages with some German people facing malnutrition and starvation.

▲ A German woman burning banknotes on a stove as they became worthless during the hyperinflation crisis of 1923

Hugo Stinnes – King of the Ruhr

Hugo Stinnes owned businesses in coal, iron and the electrical industry. During hyperinflation, Stinnes used his political connections to borrow money cheaply and buy up struggling companies. He was able to pay off his loans with worthless currency and increased his businesses. Known as the 'King of the Ruhr', by 1924 he owned 1,535 companies – about 20 per cent of German industry.

2.4 The end of the hyperinflation crisis

In the summer of 1923, the Weimar Republic faced a huge crisis. The currency had collapsed and French and Belgian troops were in the Ruhr. There were political disturbances across the country including an attempted communist uprising in Saxony, one of the German states. The survival of the Weimar Republic was remarkable, with the historian Detlev Peukert writing in 1987 that the events of 1923 show 'there are no entirely hopeless situations in history'.

A new chancellor

Gustav Stresemann became the new Chancellor of Germany in August 1923. He was Chancellor between August 1923 and November 1923 for around 100 days. He decided to follow a policy called **fulfilment** and cooperate rather than work against the Allies. He took the following steps to end the hyperinflation crisis and restore stability to Germany:

- He called off the 'passive resistance' strategy in the Ruhr and promised to **fulfil** payment of reparations.
- He reduced government spending and sacked 700,000 public employees.
- He appointed a leading financial expert called **Hjalmar Schacht** to introduce a new currency. In December 1923, a new currency called the **Rentenmark** was brought in to replace the German mark.
- He began to cooperate with countries like Britain, France and the USA to gain sympathy for Germany's economic situation.

These actions reduced inflation, helped stabilise Germany and allowed the Weimar Republic to survive the crisis of 1923.

▲ The new Rentenmark currency brought stability to Germany

What can historical interpretations tell us about the hyperinflation crisis of 1923?

Apply ▶ Exam Practice

Question 3d style

How far do you agree with Interpretation 2 about the hyperinflation crisis of 1923?

Explain your answer, using *both* interpretations and your knowledge of the historical context. **(16 marks)**

> ▶ **Interpretation 1** From *Germany 1918–45* by Richard Radway, published in 1998
>
> However, not everyone suffered from the effects of hyperinflation in 1923. Many businessmen did well. High inflation could lead to big profits, especially as the increase in wages did not keep pace with the increase in prices. Also many businessmen had borrowed money from the banks and these debts were wiped out. The rise in prices was also good for farmers. In a period of serious inflation food prices will always rise highest. People will give up buying less essential goods before they stop buying food!

> ▶ **Interpretation 2** From *The Coming of the Third Reich*, by Richard J. Evans, published in 2003
>
> At its height, the hyperinflation seemed terrifying. Money lost its meaning almost completely. Printing presses were unable to keep up with the need to produce banknotes of ever more astronomical denominations, and municipalities began to print their own emergency money, using one side of the paper only. Employees collected their wages in shopping baskets or wheelbarrows, so numerous were the banknotes needed to make up their pay packets; and immediately rushed to the shops to buy supplies before the continuing plunge in the value of money put them out of reach.

Exam Tip

Reaching a judgement (Question 3d)

Question 3d in the exam is worth 16 marks and will require you to evaluate two historical interpretations.

Focus on using your own knowledge to agree and disagree with the view in Interpretation 2.

- Explain the view in Interpretation 2 – that the hyperinflation crisis had a negative impact on the German people and support with quotations. Use your own knowledge of the hyperinflation crisis of 1923 to agree with this view.
- Explain the view in Interpretation 1 – that the hyperinflation crisis had a positive impact on German people and use this to disagree with the view in Interpretation 2 that the hyperinflation crisis had a negative impact on German people. Use your own knowledge of the hyperinflation crisis to develop and further disagree with the view in Interpretation 2.
- To achieve the highest marks, you should also explain how these views are conveyed.
- Reach a judgement about how far you agree with the view in Interpretation 2 that the hyperinflation crisis had a negative impact on the German people.

3 The 'Golden Years': the recovery of the Republic, 1924–29

Connect & Engage – Gustav Stresemann (1878–1929)

As we have seen, Gustav Stresemann was Chancellor of Germany for 100 days between August and November 1923 and helped Germany recover from hyperinflation. But who was Stresemann?

Gustav Stresemann was born in Berlin in 1878. His father ran a small bar and his family was lower middle-class, but fairly wealthy. As a young man, he became passionate about politics and joined a political party called the National Liberal Party.

Early beliefs and views

In 1907, Stresemann was elected to the Reichstag and was its youngest member at the time. He quickly gained a reputation as a skilled negotiator. He was a strong supporter of Kaiser Wilhelm II and supported the policy of 'Weltpolitik' (see page 10). Stresemann was also in favour of Germany's involvement in the First World War.

Stresemann was angered by the Treaty of Versailles of 1919. He worked hard as a politician to help rebuild Germany and improve its international standing. He became the chairman of the German People's Party but was prepared to work with other politicians for the benefit of Germany.

The 'Golden Years' of the Weimar Republic

Stresemann is the politician most identified with Germany's recovery in the 1920s. This period, 1924–29, is seen as the 'Golden Age of the Weimar Republic'. Stresemann served as Foreign Minister in 1923 and from 1924 to 1929, and was also Chancellor from August 1923 to November 1923. He was Foreign Minister for nine governments in a row. He worked hard to restore Germany's international reputation and negotiated loans from the USA in the **Dawes Plan** (1924) and the **Young Plan** (1929) to help Germany's economy. Stresemann negotiated the Locarno Treaties (1925). He also won the Nobel Peace Prize in 1926 in recognition of his achievements.

Gustav Stresemann tragically died from a series of strokes on 3 October 1929 just hours after convincing the Reichstag to approve the Young Plan. His death was not just a personal tragedy but deprived the Weimar Republic of its most able and recognisable politician.

Connect & Engage

1. Read the story of Gustav Stresemann above. What impression do you get of the kind of politician he was?
2. Check your understanding. How did Stresemann help Germany recover from the crisis of 1923?

3.1 Reasons for economic recovery

Research & Record

To what extent did the Weimar economy recover?

1. Stresemann aimed to improve the Weimar economy. Make a copy of this table and collect evidence to back up the two different interpretations while reading page 25.
2. Overall, how well do you think Stresemann solved Germany's economic problems?

The German economy recovered between 1923 and 1929	The Germany economy remained weak between 1923 and 1929

Firstly as Chancellor and then as Foreign Minister, Stresemann played a leading role in trying to improve Weimar's economy. Stresemann followed a policy called Erfüllungspolitik, which means fulfilment. He promised to pay the reparations, even though he was against the Treaty of Versailles and felt the reparations were too high. However, he wanted to fulfil the Treaty of Versailles to show its unfairness.

The German economy, 1924–29

The Dawes Plan helped the German economy to partially recover. Unemployment never fell below 1.3 million during this period and by 1929, unemployment was as high as 1.9 million. However, heavy industry recovered well and production levels in 1928 were the same as in 1913. Between 1925 and 1929, German exports rose by 40 per cent while wages rose. Increased government spending led to more schools, hospitals and roads being built.

▶ **Source A** Gustav Stresemann, the German Foreign Minister, in a speech given to The League of Nations, September 1929

The economic position is only flourishing on the surface. Germany is in fact dancing on a volcano. If the short-term loans are called in by America, a large section of our economy would collapse.

Rentenmark

Stresemann's introduction of the **Rentenmark** (see page 22) helped bring inflation under control. There was a compensation system for people who had lost their savings but it was not enough. Many people, especially the middle classes, had lost savings and they blamed the Weimar Republic for this.

Dawes Plan (1924)

Fulfilment enabled Stresemann to negotiate the Dawes Plan of 1924. The plan was named after Charles G. Dawes, an American banker. The plan said:
- The reparations were reduced in the short term to £50 million per year.
- US banks agreed to loan money to German industry. In total around £25 billion was loaned by US banks to German companies between 1924 and 1929.

The Dawes Plan gave the Allies confidence that Germany would pay the reparations. As a result, the French agreed to leave the Ruhr industrial area.

Young Plan (1929)

In August 1929, the Young Plan was agreed. It was named after American banker Owen Young. This reduced the total reparations bill and Germany would have until 1988 to pay it off. However, nationalist parties such as the Nazis and the German Nationalist Party were very angry and organised a campaign against its acceptance. Nevertheless, 85 per cent of Germans voted in favour in the referendum on the Young Plan.

Apply ▶ Exam Practice

Question 1 style

Give two things you can infer from Source A about the German economic recovery. **(4 marks)**

3.2 Germany gains international acceptance

Research & Record

To what extent did the Weimar Republic recover?

1. Stresemann's policies seemed to make Germany more stable. Make a copy of this table and collect evidence from pages 26–27 to back up the two different interpretations.
2. Overall, how stable do you think Germany was between 1924 and 1929?

Germany was stable between 1924 and 1929	Germany remained unstable between 1924 and 1929

▲ Was Germany 'dancing on a volcano' in the late 1920s?

▶ **Source B** Stresemann's speech on 10 September 1926 to the League of Nations

The German government may well speak for the great majority of the German race when it declares that it will wholeheartedly devote to the duties devolving upon the League of Nations.

Germany and international relations

After the First World War, Germany's relations with other countries were at rock bottom. As a result, Germany was not allowed to join the **League of Nations**, an international group to promote peace. As Foreign Minister, Stresemann sought to improve Germany's reputation with other countries.

The Locarno Pact (1925)

The Locarno Pact was a group of treaties signed in October 1925 between Germany, Britain, France, Belgium and Italy. Stresemann himself suggested the pact. It said that:

- Germany accepted its borders with France and Belgium as laid out by the Treaty of Versailles.
- All five countries agreed to not use force against each other.
- The five countries agreed to consider Germany joining the League of Nations.

The pact was significant because Germany was treated as an equal partner. Some nationalist groups hated the fact Stresemann had confirmed borders decided for Germany by the Treaty of Versailles.

Stresemann and Aristide Briand (France's Foreign Minister) were jointly awarded the Nobel Peace Prize in 1926 in recognition of the Locarno Treaties.

The League of Nations (1926)

In September 1926 Germany was invited to join the League of Nations. It immediately became a permanent member of the Council, making it one of the most important members.

Some opponents of the Weimar Republic felt the League of Nations was a symbol of the unpopular Treaty of Versailles. However, to Stresemann it confirmed Germany's status as a great power.

Domestic politics, 1924–29

Between 1924 and 1929 there were three elections in Germany. During this time, support for **moderate** parties grew while support for **extremist** parties like the Communists and the Nazis reduced.

Between 1924 and 1929, support for the Social Democrats increased from 100 seats (May 1924) to 153 seats (May 1928). Support for the Nazis reduced from 32 seats (May 1924) to just 12 seats (May 1928). In 1928, a Grand Coalition of the SPD (Social Democrats), German Democratic Party (DDP), German People's Party (DVP) and Centre Party (ZP) was formed under SPD leader Hermann Müller. It had support of 60 per cent of the Reichstag. It seemed like Weimar democracy was working.

Despite this, there were seven governments, and three different Chancellors between 1924 and 1929. This shows that German politics remained unstable during this time.

Presidential election (1925)

Under the Weimar Constitution, a presidential election would take place every seven years, so one was due in 1925. It was expected that Weimar President Friedrich Ebert would be re-elected. However, Ebert died of appendicitis in February 1925. The election of April 1925 resulted in **Paul von Hindenburg** from the German Nationalist Party (DNVP) being voted President.

Candidate (party)	Votes (millions)	Percentage
Paul von Hindenburg (DNVP)	14.6	48
Wilhelm Marx (ZP)	13.7	45
Ernst Thälmann (KPD – Communists)	1.9	6

▲ Results of the 1925 presidential election

Von Hindenburg was a 77-year-old conservative, nationalist and a war hero from the First World War. His election made the Weimar Republic seem strong and reliable.

Impact of foreign policy on domestic politics

In 1927, Allied troops left the west bank of the River Rhine. This was five years earlier than planned. This boosted the popularity of Stresemann's policies.

The Young Plan of 1929 gave US loans which helped Germany to pay reparations. However, it led to huge opposition from rich German businessmen. They campaigned against the Young Plan in the referendum campaign.

3.3 How stable was Germany between 1924 and 1929? Source and interpretations focus

> **Exam Tip**
>
> ### Analysing sources and interpretations (Questions 3a, b, c, d)
>
> **Step 1:** Question 3a tells you the focus of the enquiry, in this case the extent of the German recovery by 1929. All the questions will have an enquiry. Make sure you underline it in the question.
>
> **Step 2:** Read each source carefully before answering Question 3a. Annotate it (highlighting important sentences or phrases). Read what the caption says about the provenance (origins) of each source. Underline when the source was produced, its nature and by whom.
> Now answer Question 3a using the advice on page 29.
>
> **Step 3:** Read each interpretation carefully. Annotate them (highlighting important sentences or phrases). Underline the arguments of each author.
> Now answer Questions 3b, 3c and 3d.

▲ **Source C** Gustav Stresemann, the German Foreign Minister, in a speech given to the League of Nations, September 1929)

The economic position is only flourishing on the surface. Germany is in fact dancing on a volcano. If the short-term loans are called in by America, a large section of our economy would collapse.

▲ **Source D** From a German journalist, written in 1930

In comparison with what we expected after Versailles, Germany has raised herself up to shoulder the terrific burden of this peace in a way we would never have thought possible. So that today after ten years we may say with certainty 'Even so, it might have been worse'. The stage of convalescence from Versailles is a very long road to go and we have travelled it surprisingly quickly. It now shoulders the terrific burden of that peace in a way we should never have thought possible. The bad feeling of Versailles has been conquered.

▲ **Interpretation 1** From *Nazi Germany, A New History*, by K. Fischer, 1995

The middle years of the Weimar Republic, sometimes referred to as the Roaring or Golden Twenties, saw a temporary return of domestic prosperity and a concurrent relaxation in international relations ... Many western loans were made to Germany, creating an impressive boom that persuaded many that the crisis of 1923 had been resolved. Germany used the borrowed capital in two profitable ways; financing a program of public works and investing in the modernisation of industry. In 1923 German industrial output had fallen to 47 per cent of 1913 levels, but by 1929 it surpassed 1913 levels by 4 per cent.

▲ **Interpretation 2** By historian Richard Bessel

Even during the years of 'relative stabilisation' all was not well with the Weimar Republic. The profound social, economic, political and psychological destabilisation which had set in with the First World War had not really been overcome; underlying economic problems remained, and the relative political stability of Weimar's 'golden years' rested on shaky foundations.

While the two liberal parties saw their popular support dwindle and the moderate conservatives lost roughly a third of their supporters, many voters turned to special interest parties – betraying a lack of faith in a democratic politics which focused on the common good.

Apply — Exam Practice

Question 3a style

How useful are Sources C and D for an enquiry into how well Germany had recovered by 1929? Explain your answer, using Sources C and D and your knowledge of this historical context. (8 marks)

Question 3b style

Study Interpretations 1 and 2. They give different views about the extent of the German recovery by 1929.

What is the main difference between these views? Explain your answer, using details from both interpretations. (4 marks)

Question 3c style

Suggest one reason why Interpretations 1 and 2 give different views about the extent of the German recovery by 1929.

You may use Sources C and D to help explain your answer. (4 marks)

Question 3d style

How far do you agree with Interpretation 2 about the extent of the German recovery between 1924 and 1929?

Explain your answer, using *both* interpretations and your knowledge of the historical context. (16 marks)

Exam Tip

For Question 3a

Focus on content (the information in the source about the extent of the German recovery by 1929), developing using contextual knowledge and provenance (nature, origin or purpose) of the sources. Remember to try to explain how the provenance affects the utility of the content of the source.

For Question 3b

Focus on the content of these interpretations. Identify the main message of each and support these with a quotation.

For Question 3c

Focus on a reason that explains why the two interpretations are different. Consider one of the following:

- how the authors will have used difference sources to form their view (link to Sources C and D)
- how the authors will have emphasised different aspects of the history; for example, Source C focuses on the economy whereas Source D focuses on international relations.
- how the authors will have written with a different perspective; for example, the author of interpretation 1 has chosen to focus on Germany's economic recovery whereas the author of interpretation 2 has chosen to focus on the political instability that remained.

For Question 3d

Focus on analysing the views in the interpretations and use your own knowledge to agree and disagree with the view in Interpretation 2.

- Explain the view in Interpretation 2 – that Germany had not recovered by 1929 and support with quotations. Use your own knowledge of Germany between 1924 and 1929 to agree with this view.
- Explain the view in Interpretation 1 – that Germany had recovered by 1929 and use this to disagree with the view in Interpretation 2 that Germany had not recovered by 1929. Use your own knowledge of Germany between 1924 and 1929 to develop and further disagree with the view in Interpretation 2.
- To achieve the highest marks, you should also explain how these views are conveyed.
- Explain your judgement about how far you agree with the view in Interpretation 2 that Germany had not recovered by 1929.

4 Changes in society, 1924–29

Connect & Engage – Magnus Hirschfeld (1868–1935)

Magnus Hirschfeld grew up in a time when German society had very strict views on sexuality and gender.

Hirschfeld became a doctor and spent his life fighting for the rights of LGBTQ+ people. He believed everyone should be treated with equal respect no matter what their sexual orientation or gender identity. He was one of the first people to argue for gay and transgender rights.

In 1897, Hirschfeld founded the Scientific Humanitarian Committee, one of the first organisations to support LGBTQ+ rights. He carried out research on human sexuality and provided medical and psychological support for transgender people. He also campaigned to abolish a German law which made same-sex relationships between men a crime. The law said that these relationships were 'indecent activity'.

Under the Weimar government

In 1919, the Social Democratic government of Prussia gave Hirschfeld a large grant to turn his Committee into an Institute for Sexual Science. It was based in the Tiergarten District of Berlin. This gave important support and advice on sexuality and gender. His work helped to make birth control and sex counselling clinics available to people. Hirschfeld's Institute and work. The Weimar Republic's increased freedoms created a **culture** where people were excited about changing society for the better. Without this, Hirschfeld's work could never have happened.

Under the Nazis

On the morning of 6 May 1933, Magnus Hirschfeld's Institute for Sexual Science was stormed by Nazi students. The institute's records were seized and could be later used to identify LGBTQ+ people. Nazi students poured red ink over books and manuscripts. On 10 May, the Nazis carried out the Burning of the Books, which included thousands of books from Hirschfeld's library.

Hirschfeld fled Germany when the Nazis came to power but remained committed to supporting the LGBTQ+ community. His work and its impact remind us of the increase in freedom enjoyed during this period. Hirschfeld's story demonstrates the openness of German culture in the 1920s, particularly in cities like Berlin. His courage and dedication serve as an example for creating a more inclusive and compassionate world.

> ▶ **Interpretation 1** From Richard J. Evans, *The Coming of the Third Reich*
>
> Hirschfeld was the driving force behind the spread of public and private birth control and sex counselling clinics in the Weimar Republic. Not surprisingly he was repeatedly vilified by the Nationalists and the Nazis.

Connect & Engage

1. Read the story of Magnus Hirschfeld. What does his story tell you about Weimar culture in the 1920s?
2. Why do you think right-wing groups such as Nationalists and the Nazis were against his ideas?

4.1 Changes in the standard of living

> **Research & Record**
>
> **Did the standard of living improve between 1924 and 1929?**
>
> | Living standards improved | Living standards did not improve |
> |---|---|
> | | |
>
> Make your own copy of the table: record evidence of whether people's standard of living improved between 1924 and 1929 using the information on this page. Try to focus on the second order concept of similarity and difference and focus on which groups benefited and which groups lost out.
>
> Which group(s) benefited the most from the change in the standard of living between 1924 and 1929?

Work and wages

Unemployment went down between 1924 and 1929. For people with jobs, wages and working conditions improved. The working week shortened from 50 hours (1925) to 46 hours (1927). Real wages (the value of goods that wages can buy) increased by 25 per cent from 1925 to 1928. During the late 1920s, German workers were some of the best paid in Europe.

Many middle-class people did not benefit economically and many had lost out due to the hyperinflation crisis of 1923 (see pages 20–22). Most of the middle class did not experience a rise in wages and many were not able to claim welfare. Although unemployment fell, it stayed high among those who worked in professions such as the law, the civil service and teaching.

Housing

There was a shortage of housing in parts of Germany after the First World War. Article 155 of the Weimar Constitution promised suitable housing for every German. The Weimar Republic employed architects and planners to build new cost efficient housing estates. The Weimar Republic encouraged construction of new houses through direct investment, tax breaks, land grants and low-interest loans. Between 1924 and 1931, two million new homes were built, and around 200,000 homes were renovated or extended.

▶ **Source A** From the annual report of Deutsche Bank

> [The economy] is so overloaded with taxes required by the excessively expensive apparatus of the state, with over-high social payments, and particularly with the reparations sum now reaching its 'normal' level' [as laid down by the Dawes Plan] that any healthy growth is constricted.

Social reforms including unemployment insurance

The Weimar Republic raised the highest level of income tax from 4 per cent to 60 per cent. This let it change how the government looked after people:

- The Unemployment Insurance Act of 1927 created a new system of unemployment and sickness support if people could not work. The system covered 17 million workers and was the largest scheme in the world.
- Accident insurance was introduced for jobs that could make people sick, like mining.
- The working week was reduced to a maximum of 46 hours.
- There were benefits and pensions for widows and those who had been injured in the First World War.

Although these changes brought benefits, the Weimar Republic never had enough money to pay for them. Serious cuts would be made to welfare benefits when the Great Depression hit in the early 1930s.

Apply ▶ Exam Practice

Question 1 style

Give two things you can infer from Source A about the German economy in the 1920s.   (4 marks)

4.2 Changes in the position of women

Research & Record

How far did the lives of women change during the Weimar Republic?

1. Make a mind map to record your notes on changes to women's lives using the headings of Work, Politics and Leisure as you read pages 32–33.

2. When you have finished, write a conclusion to explain how much the lives of women changed. Use language from some of the key words below linked to change.

| Small-scale | Limited | Permanent | Significant |
| Widespread | Massive | Temporary | Turning point |

German social and cultural life changed dramatically in the first half of the twentieth century. The First World War affected gender balance in Germany, and this led to social changes.

Politics

Women gained equal voting rights in November 1918 and were now able to stand in elections – something that did not happen in Britain until 1928. The First World War killed so many men that in 1919 there were more women than men voting. In the 1919 election, 37 women were elected to the Reichstag. Clara Zetkin was elected a Reichstag deputy between 1920 and 1933 for the KPD. Paula Müller-Otfried was a deputy for the DNVP between 1920 and 1932, despite expressing reservations about women having the vote.

Despite women being elected to the Reichstag, this didn't bring a focus on women's issues. For some of the male politicians, the presence of women in the Reichstag made them feel more strongly against feminist issues and there was a lack of real progress.

Work

During the First World War, many women worked in jobs previously done by men. However, by the mid 1920s, the number of women in work was at pre-war levels, showing little change. Although Article 109 of the Weimar Republic gave women equality, including equal employment rights, this did not happen in reality. Women were still paid less than men for doing the same job. Many professional women still gave up work if they got married. There was also a shortage of women in important jobs. For example, there were only 33 female judges in Germany in 1933. Trade unions were very powerful and male-dominated during this time. They were often against female workers and were opposed to married women having jobs, restricting work opportunities for women.

Nevertheless, the government recognising employment rights for women was a step in the right direction. There was an increase in women working in professional jobs in education, social work and as doctors. Improvements in mass production techniques also created new job opportunities for female unskilled workers, who were mostly unmarried women.

▶ **Interpretation 2** Historian Eric D. Weitz from his book, *Weimar Germany: Promise and Tragedy* (2007)

This was, of course, an idealized image that few German women, even in Berlin, actually lived. Few women could attain Hollywood-style glamour or financial independence. In 1925, about one-third of all women worked in the paid labor force, the vast majority at low-paying factory and office jobs. The new woman was in large part a class-bound image, of middle- and upper-class women who had the independence and the means to pursue their interests and desires.

Leisure

Article 109 of the Weimar Constitution had improved women's rights. For some women, the 1920s brought new opportunities and greater independence. These 'New Women', as some came to be known, had more social freedoms. They drank more, smoked in public and paid more attention to fashions. They often wore shorter skirts and make-up. A Bubikopf (meaning little boy's hair) was a short bob cut which became a popular style among women and symbolised their freedom. For some, the 'New Woman' was a sign of modernity and progress. Friedrich Hollaender symbolised the rebellious mood of the age with his 1926 song known as 'Raus mit den Männern' meaning 'Chuck Out the Men'. It was performed by lesbian cabaret star Claire Waldorff.

Female artists like Jeanne Mammen painted the night-time scene, showing its diversity and focusing on marginalised communities. Their work portrays women in nightclubs as well as performing on stage.

There was a rise in sexual freedom in the Weimar Republic. We have already found out about Magnus Hirschfeld. Laws restricting the sale of condoms were eased in 1927 and by the early 1930s there were 1600 vending machines in public places. Sex counselling centres like Magnus Hirschfeld's offered contraceptive advice while the laws on abortion were relaxed from 1927.

However, this increase in sexual freedom was challenged by the Catholic and Protestant Churches as well as by Nationalist groups. They believed that the growing equality and independence of women threatened the traditional German family unit. Many were also concerned about the falling birth rate and the rising divorce rate during this time.

▲ German women in a bar, 1930

4.3 Cultural changes in the Weimar Republic

The Weimar Republic was known for huge cultural changes. Since Kaiser Wilhelm's era, censorship had relaxed and printing techniques had become cheaper. This allowed more ideas to spread.

Research & Record

What cultural changes took place in the Weimar Republic?

There were huge changes in art and culture in the Weimar Republic. Record these changes around the key topics.

Before 1918	Cultural changes in the Weimar Republic
Art did not portray everyday life	
Architecture was elaborate and decorative	
Cinema did not really exist	
Literature was not very political	
Theatre focused largely on events in Germany's past	

Art

Art changed greatly during the Weimar Republic. The focus was on portraying everyday life. This was known as **Neue Sachlichkeit** which means 'New Objectivity'. Key artists of this style included Max Beckmann, Otto Dix, George Grosz and Jeanne Mammen.

George Grosz had served briefly in the First World War before being discharged in 1915 after being hospitalised for sinusitis. As you can see in his painting 'Grey Day', he often portrayed people with robotic features to show that they no control over their lives. Grosz had joined the Communist Party in 1918. He was even charged with insulting the army in 1920 in one of his exhibitions.

Otto Dix lived in Berlin and Dresden in the 1920s. He was often very critical of German society. His paintings portrayed the suffering of war veterans and immorality of Germany's night life. He often contrasted the experience of war veterans with those who were benefiting during Weimar's 'Golden Age'. One of Dix's most famous paintings was called 'Metropolis'. It was a three-part painting showing three nighttime scenes from the Weimar Republic.

▲ 'Grey Day', a painting by George Grosz, 1921.
© Estate of George Grosz, Princeton, N.J. / DACS 2024

Architecture

The architect **Walter Gropius** merged the Weimar Art Academy and the Weimar School of Art and Crafts to create the State Bauhaus in Weimar. Its bohemian architecture students were both male and female and were responsible for a new type of architecture known as **Bauhaus**. One of its key principles was 'form follows function'. The style of architecture was known for its simple, clean and modern designs. They designed houses as well as simple pieces of furniture such as chairs and tables. The style made the most of modern mass production techniques to try to bring the style to a wider market. This approach was very different to the highly elaborate and decorative style before 1918.

The Törten Housing Estate in Dessau was a project developed by Walter Gropius in 1926. It was an experimental housing project. It featured affordable and efficiently designed apartments that included communal spaces and functional layouts for the working class.

The style of architecture was controversial and state funding was removed in 1924. When the Nazis came to power, Gropius had to leave Germany for the USA where he became a Professor at Harvard University. There, its legacy remained and lived on.

Cinema

Changes in technology meant that the cinema flourished after the First World War. Berlin was at the heart of the world cinema industry. Fritz Lang was a famous film director who produced the film *Metropolis* in 1926. It was a highly innovative and technically advanced film for the era. Marlene Dietrich was a famous German film star. Another popular film was called *The Cabinet of Dr Caligari,* which was one of the world's first horror films. In reality, its message was anti-war.

Literature

Literature in the 1920s become much more politicised. On the right, writers such as Ernst Junger glorified the First World War in books such as *Storm of Steel*. On the other hand, writers on the left such as Erich Remarque were anti-war. Remarque wrote a famous anti-war novel called *All Quiet on the Western Front.*

Theatre

New types of theatre productions emerged in the 1920s. They were called *Zeittheater* and *Zeitoper*. This means theatre and opera 'of the time'. The plays were noted for their realism. In Erwin Piscator's *The Salesman of Berlin* three street-sweepers were portrayed as sweeping away Germany's problems. Meanwhile Kurt Weill's *The Threepenny Opera*, which was adapted by Bertolt Brecht, became a box office hit. There was more freedom in terms of plays with actors and musicians performing vulgar songs that would never have been allowed during the rule of the Kaiser.

Nightclubs, music and cabaret

Nightclubs started becoming really popular in Germany, especially in places like Berlin. This city had a vibe of freedom and for trying new things. There were cabaret performers who sang songs that spoke out against the government. They openly talked about things related to sex. Berlin became well known for having events like transvestite balls, naked dancing and exciting nightclubs. This new freedom was welcomed by some but appalled others, such as right-wing conservatives.

Part 1: Review

> **Revision Tip**
>
> **Regularly revisit content to make it stick**
>
> You have now completed the first part of your GCSE History course. It is important to build in regular revision activities as you complete your GCSE learning. Look at the graph on page 9 which reminds you how quickly you can forget information. If you regularly revisit your key knowledge then you will be able to remember it. The revision challenges below will help you to revisit material from Part 1 of your GCSE syllabus.

Apply ▶ Recall Challenges

Key individuals

Study these individuals.

- Kaiser Wilhelm II
- Friedrich Ebert
- Gustav Stresemann
- Magnus Hirschfeld
- Rosa Luxemburg
- Wolfgang Kapp
- Paul von Hindenburg

For each one, try to answer these questions from memory. Get somebody else to test you.
- Who were they?
- What were their aims and beliefs?
- What was their impact and importance?

Key events

Study these key events.

- Spartacist Rising
- Kapp Putsch
- Treaty of Versailles
- Occupation of the Ruhr
- Hyperinflation
- Dawes Plan
- Young Plan

For each event, fill in this table to help you recall the details.

What?	When?	Who?	What happened?

Know your key words

Read the following key words and write a definition of each one. Use the glossary to help you remember some of the main words if you get stuck. Get somebody else to test you on the meaning of the key words.

The Weimar Republic, 1918–29			
Reichstag	Constitution	Reparations	Putsch
Armistice	Abdicate	Chancellor	Communism
Nationalism	Bauhaus	Culture	Hyperinflation
League of Nations	Stab in the Back Myth	November Criminals	Spartacist Rising

Exam Tip

Support your answer with specific knowledge (Question 2)

In the exam, you can improve your explanations by including relevant facts to support your arguments. For example, when answering this question:

- Do not simply say 'Germany had to pay reparations'.
- Say 'The German people disliked the Treaty of Versailles because they had to pay for war damage. This was called reparations. Germany had to pay £6.6 billion which was a lot of money.'

Apply ▶ Exam Practice

Question 2 style

For Question 2, you will have a choice of completing either 2a or 2b. Reflect which of these two questions you would decide to do. These exam questions test your understanding of Part 1. Practise them now. Use the Exam Tips in the book to help you.

> Explain why the German people felt that the Treaty of Versailles was so unfair.
>
> **You may use the following in your answer:**
> - **Diktat (Dictated Peace)**
> - **Reparations**
>
> **You must also use information of your own.** (12 marks)

> Explain why Germany was able to recover in the years 1924 to 1929.
>
> **You may use the following in your answer:**
> - **The introduction of the Rentenmark**
> - **US loans**
>
> **You must also use information of your own.** (12 marks)

Summarise

Here is a memory aid to help you remember the solutions that Gustav Stresemann came up with in the **'Golden Age'** of the Weimar Republic.

Good relations with other countries
Occupation with the Ruhr ended
Loans from the USA
Dawes Plan
Economy improved
New currency introduced

Here is another memory aid about the challenges the Weimar Republic faced between 1919 and 1923. Can you create a visual to help you remember this?

Spartacist Rising
Hyperinflation
Assassinations
Reparations
Kapp Putsch
Stab in the Back Myth

Now create your own memory aid that helps you remember Weimar culture. Aim to cover the different aspects of Weimar culture.

1 Early development of the Nazi Party, 1920–22

Connect & Engage – Adolf Hitler (1889–1945)

Adolf Hitler was born in Braunau am Inn, a small Austrian town near the German border. He did not do well in school and often got into trouble. His father, a middle-class Austrian customs official, had a difficult relationship with him and died in 1903. Following his father's death, Hitler lived in Linz, with his mother, sister and aunt. He spent his time drawing, reading and attending operas.

In 1907, two key events changed Hitler's life. His application to the Vienna Academy of Art was rejected. Secondly, his beloved mother Klara died of cancer. Hitler was 18 years old. Despite hoping to attend art college in Vienna the following year, he faced ongoing failures. He worked in various jobs, including as a painter, labourer and road sweeper, and struggled financially. It was during this time in Austria that he encountered antisemitic political ideas, which historians believe contributed to his later anti-Jewish sentiments.

The First World War

In 1913, Hitler left Vienna and moved to Munich, Germany, where he found himself when the First World War broke out. Although he was Austrian, he enlisted in the German army instead of the Austrian army. The war became a turning point for him, and he considered it a relief from the painful memories of his youth. He displayed bravery and was an excellent soldier, earning promotions and even the Iron Cross, First Class, for his courage. He was wounded twice and temporarily blinded by mustard gas towards the end of the war, during which he learned about the German Revolution and its defeat.

Believing in the Stab in the Back Myth, Hitler felt a growing resentment towards those he saw as responsible for Germany's defeat. Hitler wrote about his feelings on the war, saying, 'And so, it had all been in vain … and in vain the two million who died … Hatred grew in me, hatred for those responsible … I, for my part, decided to go into politics!'

After the war, Hitler joined a small political group called the German Workers' Party (DAP). He quickly turned it into the National Socialist German Workers' Party (NSDAP), commonly known as the Nazis. By 1933, he had risen to the position of Chancellor of Germany.

Connect & Engage

1 Read the story of Adolf Hitler's early life above. What impression do you get of what kind of person he was?
2 Are there any clues in the story as to why he wanted to get involved in politics?

1.1 The early years of the Nazi Party

> ### Research & Record
>
> **Why did people begin to support the Nazi Party, 1919–22?**
>
> Use a table like the one below to start to produce clear, well-organised notes on why people supported the Nazi Party in the early years. Use pages 39–40 to complete the table.
>
> | Identify – why did people support the Nazi Party? | Explanation – why was this? |
> |---|---|
> | The political ideas of the Nazis expressed in the Twenty-Five Point Programme | |
> | The role of the SA | |
> | Hitler's leadership | |
> | Party organisation | |

Hitler joins the German Workers' Party (DAP)

The Deutsche Arbeiterpartei (DAP) or German Workers' Party was set up by a railway mechanic and locksmith called **Anton Drexler** in January 1919. Hitler came across the party while working as an army spy. His job was keeping an eye on political groups after the First World War. More and more, Hitler found he agreed with the DAP's ideas.

On 12 September 1919, Hitler made a passionate speech and impressed Drexler. A week later, Hitler officially joined the party as member number 555. However, he wasn't the 555th member! The numbering began at 501, which shows how small the party was. Hitler quickly became the star speaker of the party. By January 1920, Hitler was in charge of propaganda and used posters to advertise political meetings held in beer halls (huge pubs – some had space for thousands of people).

The Nazi Party

In 1920, the word 'national socialist' was added to the party's name and it became the NSDAP (Nationalsozialistische Deutsche Arbeiterpartei). The word 'Nazi' came from Nationalsozialistische and quickly took hold.

The Nazis made their permanent office in Munich using it to organise the party and plan their meetings. They also published a newspaper called the *Völkischer Beobachter* (People's Observer). This helped Nazi ideas spread across Germany.

The Twenty-Five Point Programme

In February 1920, Hitler and Drexler wrote the party's **Twenty-Five Point Programme**, which listed the policies of the NSDAP. Their main policies focused on opposition to the Weimar Republic and democracy and antisemitism (being against Jewish people).

Point	Information
1	The union of all Germans to form a Greater Germany
2	Abolish the Treaty of Versailles
3	Germany needs land and colonies to feed the German people
4	German citizenship should only be granted to those of German blood. No Jewish person can be a citizen of Germany
6	Only German citizens should be allowed to vote
7	Foreign people should be deported if there are not enough resources for the German population
14	The government should have a share in the profits of major industries
17	Land can be taken from rich people by the state without paying them
23	All newspaper editors must be German, and non-German papers can only be published with government permission
24	Religious freedom for everyone as long as the views do not threaten or offend the German people
25	The creation of a strong central government for Germany to put the new programme into effect

▲ The main points of the Twenty-Five Point Programme

The role of the SA

As we have seen, politics in early 1920s Germany was extremely violent and chaotic; political parties even had their own armed forces. The Nazis created their own protection squad in 1921 led by **Ernst Röhm**. The SA (Sturmabteilung, or Stormtroopers) were known as the 'Brownshirts' due to the colour of their uniform. It became the Nazi Party's private army. Lots of ex-soldiers from the First World War chose to join them. Between 1921 and 1923, the SA disrupted other parties' political meetings especially those of left-wing parties like the Communists and the Social Democrats.

Hitler's leadership

Hitler officially became the **Führer** (leader) of the Nazi Party in July 1921. He came up with the Führerprinzip (leadership principle) which was the idea that Hitler should have complete control of the party. He created the swastika as the symbol of the Party as well as the Sieg Heil salute.

Hitler surrounded himself with his supporters to help him lead the party. The main ones were Rudolf Hess, Hermann Goering, Julius Streicher and Ernst Röhm. Streicher was an ex-soldier who founded the newspaper *Der Stürmer* in 1923, which became a Nazi newspaper.

Growth of the party

Membership of the Nazi party grew from 1,100 (June 1920) to 55,000 (November 1923). Hitler's powerful speeches were a major reason why the Nazis gained this support.

▲ 'In the Beginning Was the Word', a painting by Hermann Otto Hoyer, c.1937, showing Hitler speaking

Apply ▶ Exam Practice

Question 1 style

Give two things you can infer from Source A about Hitler's political views. **(4 marks)**

▶ **Source A** From a letter written by Adolf Hitler in 1921

During the communist attempt to take over in Munich I remained in the army ... In my talks as an education officer, I attacked the bloodthirsty Red dictatorship ... In 1919, I joined the German Workers' Party, which then had seven members, and I believed that I had found a political movement in keeping with my own ideas.

Apply — Exam Practice

Question 3a style

Study Sources B and C.

How useful are Sources B and C for an enquiry into the Nazi Party in the early 1920s?
Explain your answer, using Sources B and C and your knowledge of the historical context. **(8 marks)**

> **Source B** The pledge of loyalty and obedience taken by members of the SA
>
> As a member of the NSDAP, I pledge myself by its storm flag to:
> - be always ready to stake life and limb in the struggle for the aims of the movement
> - give absolute military obedience to my military superiors and leaders
> - bear myself honourably in and out of service.

> **Source C** A member of the Nazi Party describing one of Hitler's speeches in 1922
>
> My critical faculty was swept away. Leaning forward as if he were trying to force his inner self into the consciousness of all these thousands, he was holding the masses and me with them, under a hypnotic spell by the sheer force of his belief ... I forgot everything but the man; then glancing around, I saw that his magnetism was holding these thousands as one.

Exam Tip

Evaluating usefulness of sources (Question 3a)

This is a source-based question.

- You have to analyse both sources carefully, identifying what they tell you and explaining why they are useful.
- You have just over 10 minutes to answer this question in the exam. One paragraph for each source is enough for a high-level answer.
- You should focus on how they are useful for the enquiry in the question.
- The examiner does not want you to highlight the problems with the sources. For example, Source B is very useful because its provenance as the pledge that SA members took in the 1920s gives us an insight into the role of the SA. We can infer they had to be very disciplined when it says 'absolute military obedience'.
- In the rest of your paragraph, develop and support your argument by referring to the content, provenance and your wider knowledge of the enquiry and make a judgement on how useful it is.

C The content of the source

Before you begin to write, highlight/annotate the key information in the source.

K Your own knowledge of the period

You will need to bring in your own knowledge to explain how the source is useful for the enquiry in the question. Remember that:

- The SA was created in 1920 to give the Nazis their own private army and attracted many ex-soldiers from the First World War.
- Hitler's public speaking ability was an important reason for Nazi support right from the early years of the Nazi Party.

P The provenance of the source

Remember that both sources are from the early 1920s. The source, therefore, gives us an excellent insight into the early years of the Nazi Party. For example:

Source C is useful because it is written by an early member of the Nazi Party who can give us an insight into the powerful impact of speeches. From this, we can infer that speeches were an important method of persuading people to join the Nazi Party.

Connect & Engage

Connect the information on the early years of the Nazi Party with what you already know about the Weimar Republic between 1919 and 1923.

Explain why the Nazis would have been against the Weimar Republic. Think about the following:

- The Stab in the Back Myth
- The Treaty of Versailles
- The threat of communism
- The Weimar Constitution and democracy

2 The Munich Putsch and the Nazi Party, 1923–28

2.1 The reasons for and events of the Munich Putsch

Research & Record

Why did the Munich Putsch fail?

Read pages 42–43 and answer the following questions.

1. Why did Hitler attempt a putsch in 1923?
2. Identify reasons why the Munich Putsch failed. Find examples of the following:
   a. bad planning
   b. mistakes made by Hitler and Ludendorff during the putsch
   c. the reactions of von Kahr and von Lossow
   d. the reactions of the German government
3. What do you think was the main reason why the putsch failed? Write a conclusion in your notebook.

What did the Nazis want to achieve by the Munich Putsch?

Wolfgang Kapp was not the only right-wing politician who tried to overthrow the Weimar Republic by force. By 1923, the Nazis had grown in power and Adolf Hitler and General Ludendorff made their own attempt. This is called the **Munich Putsch**. Ludendorff was a popular First World War hero who had been involved in the Kapp Putsch.

Hitler and the Nazi Party believed that democracy made weak governments. Instead, they thought that there should be one political party, with one leader. They planned to take over the government and set up General Ludendorff as leader. Hitler and the Nazis were inspired by a similar uprising in Italy in 1922 when Benito Mussolini had taken power after his March on Rome. The Nazis thought they could do the same.

Why did Hitler believe his putsch could succeed?

The starting place for Hitler and Ludendorff's putsch was in Munich, the largest city in a part of Germany called Bavaria.

- The Nazi Party was popular in Bavaria.
- Germany was in chaos due to hyperinflation.
- By 1923, the Nazi Party had 55,000 members.
- The SA were now a strong fighting force led by Ernst Röhm.
- In Bavaria the Weimar Republic was not popular.
- Bavaria's leader, Gustav von Kahr, was right-wing. It seemed like he wanted to rebel against the Weimar Government. Von Kahr and his officials protected armed groups (including Freikorps) who opposed the Republic.
- Von Kahr had the support of the Bavarian part of the army, led by General Otto von Lossow. Even though the Treaty of Versailles said that the German army could not have more than 100,000 men, it was estimated that there were at least 42,000 armed men in Bavaria.
- Hitler believed that von Kahr, von Lossow and Ludendorff would help him launch an attack on the government.

Connect & Engage

The Munich Putsch was another example of a rebellion against the Weimar Republic. Compare the putsch to the Spartacist Rising and the Kapp Putsch (see pages 18–19). Which posed the greatest threat to Weimar? Think about the following to help you:

- The leadership
- How much support it had
- How organised it was
- How close it came to overthrowing the Weimar Republic
- How the Weimar Republic defeated it

42

The events of the Munich Putsch

8 November

Otto von Lossow and Gustav von Kahr are speaking at a meeting of 2000 right-wing supporters in a beer hall in Munich.

Hitler and 600 of his SA Stormtroopers burst into the meeting. They state that they are starting a revolution to overthrow the government of Germany.

Holding a gun, Hitler forces von Kahr and von Lossow into a side room. They are forced to say that they will support a march on Berlin to overthrow the government and Ludendorff will take over as leader of Germany.

After von Lossow and von Kahr agree to support Hitler's plans, they are allowed to leave the beer hall.

9 November

The German government responds quickly. President Ebert declares a state of emergency. Von Lossow and the army are ordered to crush the revolt.

9 November (continued)

Von Kahr and von Lossow decide not to join the putsch. Instead, they issue a statement saying that they oppose the putsch.

Despite this setback, Hitler and Ludendorff continue with their plans and march to the centre of Munich. Ludendorff believes that some soldiers in the German army will support him.

2000 armed Nazis start marching towards a military base in Munich. However, they are stopped by armed police and Bavarian soldiers from the German army.

A shot is fired, probably by a Nazi, and the police fire back. Most Nazis fall to the ground and take cover. Fourteen Nazis are killed, including the person standing next to Hitler. Ludendorff continues to march towards the police and is arrested. Hitler flees from the scene.

11 November

Hitler is arrested and the Nazi Party is banned.

February 1924

Hitler and Ludendorff are placed on trial for treason, which carries the death penalty. During the trial, Hitler makes a speech attacking the Weimar Government. The judges are sympathetic to his views. He is sentenced to serve five years in prison.

Ludendorff is not even sent to prison. They accept his statement that he had only been present by accident.

December 1924

Hitler is released from prison after only nine months. But, by this point, the Nazi Party has almost broken up.

2.2 The consequences of the Munich Putsch

How did the Munich Putsch change Hitler's ideas?

Hitler used his trial to make long political speeches that were reported in lots of newspapers. This helped him become well known across Germany. Hitler was sent to prison and the Nazi Party was banned. While he was in prison, he realised that taking power in Germany through armed revolution was not going to work (see Source A on page 45).

Mein Kampf

Hitler used his time in prison to gather together his political thoughts. He wrote them down in his book **Mein Kampf** which was published in 1925. It was over 700 pages long. His main ideas were as follows:

- There should be one strong leader to make all the decisions.
- The **Aryans** are the 'Master Race'.
- All other races are inferior.
- Jewish people are the most inferior of all.
- All German-speaking peoples should be united in one country.
- Communism must be destroyed.
- **Lebensraum** (living space) must be gained to create a greater Germany. To do this the army must be rebuilt and used to invade land in Eastern Europe.
- The Treaty of Versailles should be abolished.
- Power should be taken legally: by winning votes.

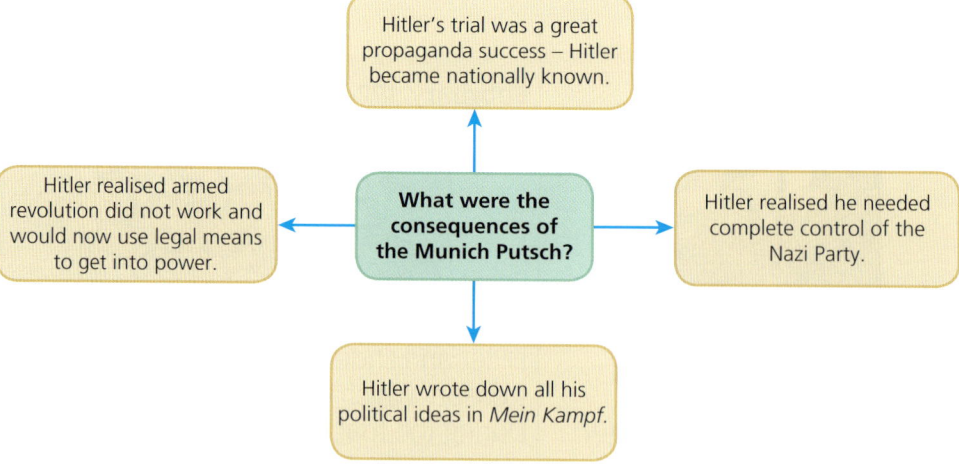

Apply ▶ Exam Practice

Question 1 style

Give two things you can infer from Source A about Hitler's political ideas after the Munich Putsch. (4 marks)

> **Source A** Karl Ludecke recalls visiting Hitler in the Landsberg Prison in 1924. This is what Hitler said:
>
> When I resume active work, it will be necessary to follow a new policy. Instead of working to achieve power by armed conspiracy, we shall have to hold our noses and enter parliament against the Catholic and communist members. If out-voting them takes longer than out-shooting them, at least the results will be guaranteed by their own constitution! Any lawful process is slow.

Apply ▶ Exam Practice

Question 3b style

Study Interpretations 1 and 2.

They give different views about the success of the Munich Putsch. What is the main difference between these views?

Explain your answer, using details from both interpretations. (4 marks)

Question 3c style

Suggest one reason why Interpretations 1 and 2 give different views about the success of the Munich Putsch.

You may use Sources A and B to help explain your answer. (4 marks)

> **Source B** Hitler's announcement at the beginning of the Munich Putsch on 9 November 1923
>
> Proclamation to the German people! The Government of the November Criminals in Berlin has today been deposed. A provisional German National Government has been formed, which consists of General Ludendorff, Adolf Hitler and Colonel von Seisser.
>
> *Colonel Hans Ritter von Seisser was the head of the Bavarian State Police in 1923

> **Interpretation 1** By journalist and historian William Shirer writing in the 1960s
>
> Hitler was shrewd enough to see that his trial would provide a new platform from which he could … for the first time make his name known far beyond the confines of Bavaria and indeed Germany itself … By the time it ended … Hitler had transformed defeat into triumph … impressed the German people by his eloquence and the fervour of his nationalism, and emblazoned his name on the front pages of the world.

> **Interpretation 2** By historian Richard J Evans, in *The Coming of the Third Reich*, published in 2003
>
> For half a minute the air was filled with whizzing bullets as both sides let fly. Göring fell, shot in the leg; Hitler dropped, or was pushed, to the ground, dislocating his shoulder. Altogether, fourteen marchers were shot dead, and four policemen. As the police moved in to arrest Ludendorff, Streicher, Röhm and many others, Göring managed to get away, fleeing first to Austria, then Italy before settling in Sweden … Hitler was taken off, his arm in a sling, [and] was arrested on 11 November. The putsch had come to an ignominious [shameful] end.

2.3 Reorganisation of the Nazi Party, 1924–28

Research & Record

How did Hitler reorganise the Nazi Party between 1924 and 1928?

Read the information on pages 46–47 and make notes to answer the question above. Use the following categories to guide you:

- The relaunch of the Nazis after Hitler's release from prison
- The Bamberg Conference
- Party organisation

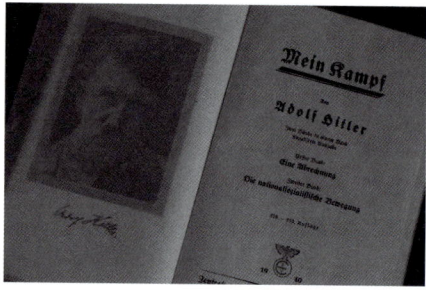

▲ Mein Kampf

Hitler's release from prison

Adolf Hitler was let out of prison on 20 December 1924. On 16 February 1925, the ban on the Nazi Party was lifted. This shows that there was still sympathy for the Nazis' ideas in 1920s Germany. Just 11 days later, Hitler restarted the Nazi Party.

Apply ▶ Recall Challenge

Which of the following ideas were included in Hitler's book *Mein Kampf*? You can use Source C below to help you complete this task or look back at the information on page 44.

01	Lebensraum (living space) in the East for German people
02	The Nazis must take power by force as quickly as possible
03	Democracy is the correct form of government for Germany
04	Germany needs a strong and powerful leader
05	All German-speaking people should be united in one country
06	Fulfil the terms of the Treaty of Versailles
07	The Aryans are the master race
08	Hitler believed there was a Jewish race and that Jewish people were inferior
09	Destroy the Treaty of Versailles
10	Defeat communism
11	Take power by legal methods

▶ **Source C** From Adolf Hitler's *Mein Kampf*, published in 1925

The German people must be assured the territorial area which is necessary for it to exist on earth ... People of the same blood should be in the same Reich (German Empire) ... Germany will either become a World Power or will not continue to exist at all ... The future goal of our foreign policy will be an Eastern policy which will have in view the acquisition of such territory as is necessary for our German people.

Nazi Party strategy and the Bamberg Conference

The failure of the Munich Putsch led to a change in approach with Hitler wanting to take power 'legally'. Some in the party disagreed and still wished to take power by force.

The Bavarian Nazis in the south preferred more nationalist ideas and the Nazis in the north liked more socialist policies that would benefit working-class people (as long as they were Aryans). One person who argued with Hitler a lot was Gregor Strasser, a northern Nazi who had helped increase support for the party in big cities in the north like Berlin.

Hitler decided to hold a meeting of the Nazi Party in 1926. He was aiming to unite both sides of the party. He held it in Bamberg, a town in Bavaria. Holding the conference in the south meant there were more southern Nazis at the meeting. Hitler let Gregor Strasser speak, but then he made a long and inspiring speech saying that Strasser's more socialist ideas were communist. This speech helped Hitler to unite the nationalist and socialist wings of the Nazi Party and made it clear that he was the leader of the party. However, he did have to accept some socialist ideas within the Twenty-Five Point Programme (see page 39). There were still some tensions that would not be fully resolved until June 1934 on the **Night of the Long Knives**.

▲ Adolf Hitler addressing a meeting of the Nazis in Munich in 1925. On the right are Gregor Strasser and Heinrich Himmler

Party reorganisation

Hitler also reorganised the Nazi Party. Germany was divided into regions called **Gaue**. Each region was controlled by a **Gauleiter** (regional leader). The Gauleiter for Berlin was Joseph Goebbels, who became a strong supporter of Hitler after the **Bamberg Conference**. He focussed on propaganda and created a newspaper called *Der Angriff* (The Attack). Goebbels would be put in charge of propaganda in 1930.

Hitler also successfully raised money for the Nazis from rich businessmen.

New Party organisations

The Nazis also started new organisations like the Hitler Youth, the Nazi Teachers' Association and the Order of German Women. Making organisations for specific groups of people helped to increase Nazi membership.

In 1925, Hitler ordered the creation of another organisation: the SS.

The SS:
- started out as Hitler's personal bodyguard
- swore complete loyalty to Hitler
- had 200 members in 1929
- was created because the SA had become so large (in 1930 there were 400,000 members).

While the SS started as an organisation of elite bodyguards, they took on a much bigger role after the Nazis came to power.

Hitler also removed Ernst Röhm as leader of the SA in 1925. Röhm did not return to the Nazi Party until 1930.

By 1928, Hitler's position as leader was secure, the Nazi Party was well organised and more and more people were joining.

Year	Membership
1925	27,000
1926	49,000
1927	72,000
1928	108,000

▲ Nazi membership 1925–28

2.4 Reasons for limited support for the Nazi Party, 1924–28

Research & Record

Why did the Nazis have limited support 1924–28?

Use a table like this to explain why the Nazis had limited support between 1924 and 1928.

You will need to add to your table after reading pages 48 and 49.

Leave column 3 (your evaluation) until you have completed all reasons.

Reason	Explanation: How did it lead to the Nazis having limited support?	Evaluation: How important was it for the Nazis having limited support?
Weimar stability		
International standing		
President von Hindenburg		
Weakness of the Nazis		

Despite increasing members and support, the Nazis struggled to gain votes in the 1920s. By May 1928, it seemed like the Nazi Party wasn't going to become important any time soon.

There were various reasons for the limited support the Nazis received:
- The loans that Stresemann had secured meant the Weimar Republic's economy was more stable. Many people were much better off.
- Welfare schemes to support people who were unwell or unemployed were popular.
- Stresemann's policies as foreign minister had helped to restore Germany's reputation with other countries. This made the policies popular.
- Paul von Hindenburg became president in 1925. He was a physically imposing man and had a legendary reputation for winning the Battle of Tannenburg in 1914. He was a popular figurehead and helped increase support for the Weimar government.

Election date	Nazi seats in Reichstag	% of vote
May 1924	32	6.5
Dec 1924	14	3.0
May 1928	12	2.6

▲ Support for the Nazis in elections, 1924–28

▶ **Source D** A confidential report on the Nazis by the Weimar Republic's Interior Ministry, July 1927

A numerically insignificant ... radical-revolutionary splinter group incapable of exerting any noticeable influence on the great mass of the people and the course of political events.

President von Hindenburg

Paul von Hindenburg won the 1925 Presidential election (see page 27).

The weakness of the Nazis

The Nazis did get a few more votes in 1928. People like farmers liked their policies that supported smaller farms. However, bigger groups, like working-class people in large cities such as Hamburg or Berlin, weren't really interested in the Nazis. Because the Weimar Republic was doing well, Nazi messaging seemed unimportant. Not many people were interested in blaming Jewish people for Germany's problems, when, for lots of people, there didn't seem to be many big problems. It was hard to argue that Germany needed a single strong leader when Germany seemed fine without one. The Weimar Republic also tried to control the Nazi Party; for example, Hitler was banned from making speeches in public in Bavaria until 1927. Overall, when the economy was doing well, the Nazis gained little support from the poorest in society.

Exam Tip

Explaining why (Question 2)

Your exam will have a question that asks you to explain an event in history.

Think before you write using the **3Ds**.

Decode the question and work out the focus of the question.

Staying focused on the question is crucial. Including information that is not relevant or writing about the wrong topic wastes time and gains no marks. Here's how to 'decode' a question.

What are the command words?
The question starts 'Explain why'. You need to explain at least one reason.

What is the conceptual focus?
The historical concept is cause and effect. Focus on explaining why the Nazis were less popular in the years 1924 to 1928 and support with examples from your knowledge.

> **Explain why** the Nazis received limited support in the years 1924 to 1928.
> You may use the following information in your answer:
> • President von Hindenburg
> • US loans
> You must also use information of your own. **(12 marks)**

What is the content focus?
Focus on the limited support the Nazis received at this time. Mentioning details about, for example, the Bamberg Conference will waste time. The Bamberg Conference is not related to how much support the Nazis received during 1924–1928, so it will not get you marks.

How many marks are available?
'12 marks' indicates you should spend about 18 minutes on the question and write no more than three paragraphs (one per aspect of supporting knowledge).

Decide how are you going to organise your answer.

For this question, aim to include three paragraphs. The first two paragraphs can link to the two bullet points. The third paragraph could focus on the Nazis themselves and that their policies did not seem relatable for many people at this time.

Develop your answer – make sure you explain and support the points you make.

Remember to back up your points with evidence. For example, you could explain that the Nazis did not seem to have national support as they were mainly based in Bavaria and hadn't spread their presence across the country.

3 The growth in support for the Nazis, 1929–32

3.1 The growth of unemployment – its causes and impact

Research & Record

What were the causes and the impact of unemployment on the German people?

1. Read the information on pages 50–51. Make a detailed mind map of what caused unemployment and all the different ways in which unemployment affected the German people.
2. Cover up your notes and see if you can recall **ten** different effects of the Great Depression. Test yourself with a learning partner.

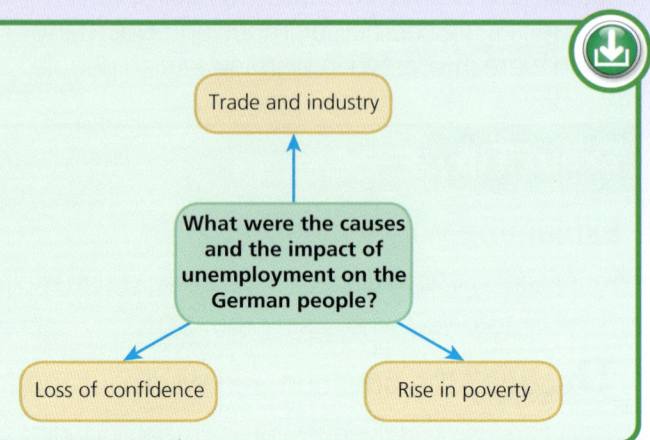

Revision Tip

Make mind maps and diagrams to help you recall information

Making mind maps, diagrams or flow charts like the one on this page can help you recall and remember information. Practise the following to help you revise:

- Read the diagram carefully. Try to redraw it again from memory.
- Compare your diagram to the one in the book and add in the details that you missed.
- Practise this revision technique regularly to help you remember information.

On 24 October 1929, exactly three weeks after Gustav Stresemann died, the American stock market collapsed. As many stock exchanges were based on Wall Street in New York, it became known as the **Wall Street Crash**. The impact of the American economic collapse would be felt around the world, but especially in Germany, leading to the **Great Depression**.

How the Wall Street Crash led to the growth of unemployment in Germany

1. The Wall Street Crash in October 1929 saw a sudden massive decrease in the values of shares on the New York Stock Exchange. It wiped 10 billion dollars off the value of major American companies.

2. American companies went bust and banks lost money. Between 1924 and 1929 American banks had lent Germany a lot of money as part of the Dawes and Young Plans. Germany had spent the money paying reparations and growing German businesses. Because the American banks had lost so much money in the Wall Street Crash, they suddenly wanted their money back.

3. German businesses were unable to finance themselves so began to reduce production, lower wages and sack workers. Many were forced to close.

4. Businesses in Germany struggled to make enough money to stay open. Many failed. This meant that unemployment in Germany increased and wages decreased. Industrial production fell by 60%.

5. A banking crisis in the summer of 1931 led to five banks shutting down. The German economy lost more and more money, and so more and more people lost their jobs. This meant they didn't have any money to spend, so businesses made less money and more people lost their jobs.

6. By 1932, there were 6 million unemployed people – one third of German workers.

How did the growth of unemployment impact on the German people?

Loss of confidence
Like hyperinflation, the Great Depression shook people's confidence in the Weimar government's ability to deal with the economy. It made many people stop trusting democracy.

Trade and industry
The Great Depression led to a decline in world trade. Suddenly nobody wanted German exports like steel, machinery and chemcials. Exports fell by 55 per cent and over 50,000 businesses went bankrupt between 1930 and 1932. With far fewer people buying their products, industries started to make less. They didn't need as many workers, and more people lost their jobs. In 1932, industrial production was only 58 per cent of what it had been in 1929.

A rise in poverty
The number of registered unemployed people was up to 6 million by early 1933. The true number could well have been as high as 9 million. In particular, many women lost their jobs and did not register as unemployed. Those workers who kept their jobs were working shorter hours and for less pay. Poverty dramatically increased which led to people losing their homes. Some homeless people lived in camps on the edge of towns and cities. Large crowds of unemployed young people were kept occupied with open-air games of chess and cards. Historians estimate that up to 23 million German people were directly affected by unemployment due to wage earners losing their jobs and not being able to support their families. Although the Weimar Republic did have an extensive welfare programme, this could not support all of those affected as the government ran out of money.

Farming
Wages and incomes within farming fell rapidly. Many farms were sold off. Agricultural prices in 1932 were 77 per cent of what they had been in 1913. Many farmers who rented their lands were forced to leave their homes. By 1932, 18,000 farmers had gone bankrupt, leading to unemployment and poverty in the countryside.

Crime
There was a huge increase in crime especially among young people. Some young people joined gangs, leading to an increase in violence on the streets. Both the Communists and the Nazis recruited young people for their military-style groups, resulting in violence and tension on the streets.

Finance and the banking crisis of 1931
In the summer of 1931, five major German banks closed down. One of the banks called the Danatbank was led by the well-known Jewish banker Jakob Goldschmidt. Hitler and the Nazis seized on this in wrongly blaming Jewish people for the economic depression. The failure of the five banks made it even harder for people and businesses to borrow money, further worsening unemployment.

▲ A desperate family in Germany c1930

Apply ▶ Exam Practice

Question 1 style

Give two things you can infer from Source A about the impact of the Great Depression on Germany. (4 marks)

> ▶ **Source A** An unemployed 21-year-old printer from Essen writing in the autumn of 1932
>
> After long, planless wanderings from city to city my path took me to the port of Hamburg. But what a disappointment! Here was yet more misery, more unemployment than I had expected, and my hopes of getting work here were dashed. What should I do? Without relatives here, I had no desire to become a vagabond [beggar].

3.2 The growth in support for the German Communist Party (KPD)

The German Communist Party (Kommunistische Partei Deutschlands) was formed just before the Spartacist Rising of 1919. Ernst Thälmann became leader in 1925 and abandoned their plan for a revolution. Instead, he sought to win votes in elections. In 1925, Thälmann was a presidential candidate and gained 1.9 million votes (6.36 per cent). As you can see from the table, the Communist Party steadily increased its support through the 1920s and into the early 1930s. In the 1932 Presidential election, Thälmann gained 4.9m votes (13.2 per cent) in the first round – although Adolf Hitler gained 30.1 per cent of the vote in the election eventually won by von Hindenburg.

The KPD was becoming more popular among unskilled workers and unemployed people. This was because they promised to redistribute wealth to the poor from the rich. They also promised more power for workers such as strengthening the power of trade unions. This appealed to many voters who had lost their jobs and could not even afford enough food to eat. The KPD organised rent strikes in working-class areas and were well supported in places like Wedding, part of Berlin. They used propaganda posters to gain support and had their own military-style organisation, the Red Front-Fighters' League, to help increase their support. This was all effective. Their national membership increased from 117,000 (1929) to 360,000 (1932). Their seats in the Reichstag increased from 77 in September 1930 to 100 in November 1932.

> 'Is the government going to fall? Is Hitler going to follow, or communism?'
>
> ▲ Victor Klemperer, a conservative moderate, writing in July 1931

▲ A 1930s KPD propaganda poster

Date of election	% of votes	Seats in Reichstag
June 1920	2.1	4
May 1924	12.6	62
Dec 1924	8.9	45
May 1928	10.6	54
Sept 1930	13.1	77
July 1932	14.3	89
Nov 1932	16.9	100
March 1933	12.3	81

▲ Communist support in the Reichstag

3.3 Reasons for growth in support for the Nazi Party

Research & Record

Why did Nazi support increase in the 1930s?

Use a table like this to explain why Nazi support increased in the 1930s.

You will need to add to your table after reading pages 53–55 so leave lots of space. Leave column 3 (your evaluation) until you have completed all reasons.

Reason	Explanation How did it lead to Nazi support increasing?	Evaluation How important was it for Nazi support increasing?
Unemployment and the economy		
Anti-communism		
The Nazis and conservative ideas		
The appeal of Adolf Hitler		
Propaganda		
The work of the SA		

In 1928, the Nazi Party had just 12 seats in the Reichstag. By the election of July 1932, the Nazis were the largest party in the Reichstag with 230 seats. Although their support fell back by November 1932, they remained the most popular political party in Germany in what were, for the most part, free and fair elections. Well over 13 million Germans voted for the Nazis in July 1932 compared to just 810,000 in May 1928.

	May 1928	Sept 1930	July 1932	Nov 1932
Nazi Party (NSDAP)	12	107	230	196
Communists (KPD)	54	77	89	100
Social Democrats (SPD)	153	143	133	121

▲ Reichstag election results 1928–32

Unemployment and the economy

Although some working-class people voted for the Communists, the Nazi Party also appealed to other working-class voters, many of whom were unemployed. As so many were affected by unemployment, the Nazis came up with the promise of 'Arbeit und Brot' (Work and Bread) as a catchy slogan to gain support and this was central to their campaign. In the 1932 presidential election the Nazis produced a distinctive poster called 'Hitler: Unsere Letzte Hoffnung' (Hitler: Our Last Hope). As we have seen, the Weimar Republic was unable to solve the problems of the Great Depression. In addition, many middle-class people had been affected by unemployment and the economic problems. Therefore, the Nazis used these very clear political messages to promise an end to the problem of unemployment.

▲ Work and Bread election poster

The Nazis' appeal to conservatives

Many conservative people felt there had been a moral decline during the Weimar Republic. They did not like the sexual openness of 1920s Weimar and wanted a return to 'traditional family values' promised by the Nazis. Farmers liked the Nazi promise of 'blood and soil' which idealised traditional German peasant-farming communities.

Anti-communism

Many people in Germany feared communism, especially the wealthy elites and middle-class professionals such as doctors, teachers, lawyers and business people. The Communists wanted to end private ownership of land as had happened in Russia after the Communist Revolution of 1917. In addition, the Nazis' military-style organisation, the SA, clashed with the Communists in the streets. Hitler's promise to be a strong leader and crush communism appealed to many. Rich industrialists like Fritz Thyssen even supported the Nazis financially due to their fear of communism. This strengthened the idea that only the Nazis could stop the Communists getting into power.

The appeal of Hitler

In the final few days of the 1932 presidential election campaign, the poster below was made. Its simple image and single word – 'Hitler' – sums up how well known Hitler was in 1932 and how important he was to Nazi success.

Presidential campaign

Hitler rose to national fame in his campaign to become President of the Weimar Republic in March–April 1932. The Nazis used modern technology within this presidential campaign. Using a plane to travel allowed Hitler to visit up to five different German cities each day. Although Hitler did not become president, the presidential campaign led to a huge increase in votes for the Nazi party in the July 1932 election.

Candidate	Number of votes
Paul von Hindenburg	19.3m
Adolf Hitler (Nazi Party)	13.4m
Ernst Thälmann (Communist Party)	3.7m votes

▲ The results of the second round of voting in the 1932 Presidential election

Hitler's speeches

Hitler practised the art of public speaking. He presented himself as the saviour of Germany with a mission to build a new Germany. He captivated audiences with his speeches. His timing, expression and the content of his speeches helped convert people to Nazism.

Hitler's image

Hitler's image was central to the Nazi message. He was always portrayed as a strong and powerful leader who would solve Germany's problems and he often dressed in an SA uniform to strengthen this image. His promise to remove the hated Treaty of Versailles and make Germany a powerful nation again appealed to many nationalists. Many abandoned the traditional German conservative party, the DNVP, to vote for Hitler.

Apply ▶ Exam Practice

Question 1 style

Give two things you can infer from Source B about the speaking skills of Adolf Hitler. (4 marks)

▶ **Source B** A Nazi supporter called Otto Strasser describes the power of Hitler's speeches

Adolf Hitler enters a hall. He sniffs the air. For a minute he gropes, feels his way, senses the atmosphere. Suddenly he bursts forth. His words go like an arrow to their target, he touches each private wound on the raw, liberating the mass unconscious, expressing its innermost aspirations, telling it what it most wants to hear.

Propaganda

Joseph Goebbels was in charge of Nazi propaganda. Goebbels made use of technology such as loudspeakers, radio broadcasts and films. The Nazis also used lots of propaganda posters like the one on the right so the people of Germany would know what the Nazi policies were.

There were several key themes to the propaganda that the Nazis used:

The cult of the Führer

Adolf Hitler was portrayed as a saviour-like figure who could solve Germany's problems such as unemployment and save Germany from communism. He was presented as a strong and powerful leader who would restore Germany's greatness.

Volksgemeinschaft (national community)

This was the idea of creating a community based on race. The community would not include people that the Nazis regarded as racially inferior, such as Jewish people. In addition, the Nazis blamed Jewish people for many of Germany's problems in their propaganda as shown in Source C.

Nationalism

The Nazis used ideas like the **Dolchstosslegende** (Stab in the Back Myth) in their propaganda. They referred to Weimar politicians as 'November Criminals' and promised to destroy the Treaty of Versailles and return Germany to being a powerful country.

The work of the SA

Membership of the Sturmabteilung (SA) increased dramatically in the early 1930s with many unemployed young men joining. By 1933, it had 500,000 members. In January 1931, Hitler re-appointed Ernst Röhm as leader of the SA. The SA gave protection to Nazi speakers and helped to deliver propaganda leaflets. Above all, with their uniform and marches, it seemed like the SA could bring order to the streets and protection from communism. The Nazis also intimidated other opponents of the Nazis. Although some people found their violence off-putting, for the most part the SA helped the Nazis to win more electoral support.

> ▶ **Interpretation 2** Ben Walsh in *GCSE Modern World History*, published in 1996
>
> The Nazis won increased support after 1929 due to Hitler. He was their greatest campaigning asset. He was a powerful speaker and was years ahead of his time as a communicator. He travelled by plane on a hectic tour of rallies all over Germany. He appeared as a dynamic man of the moment, the leader of a modern party with modern ideas. At the same time, he was able to appear to be the man of the people, someone who knew and understood the people and their problems. Nazi support rocketed.

▲ **Source C** Nazi election poster. The banner says, 'National Socialist German Workers Party'. The snake is linked to the Treaty of Versailles, unemployment, communism, lies and terror, Bolshevism [Russia Communist Party] and Jewish people.

> 'We must struggle with ideas, but if necessary also with fists'
> Adolf Hitler

> ▶ **Interpretation 1** Geoff Layton in *Democracy and Nazism: Germany 1918–1945*, published in 2019
>
> The Great Depression transformed the Nazis into a mass movement. Admittedly, 63 per cent of Germans never voted for them, but 37 per cent did, so the Nazis became by far the strongest party in a multi-party democracy. The depression had led to such profound social and economic hardship that it created an environment of discontent, which was easily exploited by the Nazis.

▶ **Source D** Adapted from the diary of Luise Solmitz. Solmitz was a schoolteacher who was writing about attending a meeting in Hamburg where Hitler was speaking.

There stood Hitler in a simple black coat, looking over the crowd of 120,000 people of all classes and ages … a forest of swastika flags unfurled, the joy of this moment showed itself in a roaring salute … The crowd looked up to Hitler with touching faith, as their helper, their saviour, their deliverer from unbearable distress … He is the rescuer of the scholar, the farmer, the worker and the unemployed.

▶ **Source E** From 'A Fairytale of Christmas', a short story written in 1931 by Rudolf Leonhard, a member of the Communist Party (KPD). Leonhard was writing about the unemployed in Germany during the Great Depression.

No one knew how many of them there were. They completely filled the streets … They stood or lay about in the streets as if they had taken root there. The streets were grey, their faces were grey, and even the hair on their heads and the stubble on the cheeks of the youngest there was grey with dust and their adversity.

▲ **Source F** A 1932 Nazi election poster. It reads 'Women! Millions of men without work. Millions of children without a future. Save the family. Vote Adolf Hitler!'

Apply ▶ Exam Practice

Question 3a style

Study Sources D and E.

How useful are Sources D and E for an enquiry into the reasons for the growth in support for the Nazi Party between 1930 and 1932?

Explain your answer, using Sources D and E and your knowledge of the historical context. (8 marks)

Question 3b style

Study Interpretations 1 and 2. They give different views about why the Nazis increased their support between 1930 and 1932.

What is the main difference between these views?

Explain your answer, using details from both interpretations. (4 marks)

Question 3c style

Suggest one reason why Interpretations 1 and 2 give different views about why the Nazis increased their support by 1932.

You may use Sources D and E to help explain your answer. (4 marks)

Question 3d style

How far do you agree with Interpretation 2 about why the Nazis increased their support between 1930 and 1932?

Explain your answer, using *both* interpretations and your knowledge of the historical context. (16 marks)

Exam Tip

Analysing sources and interpretations (Questions 3a, b, c, d)

Look again at the advice on how to approach these types of questions on page 29.

Remember to

- explain how each source is useful considering their content, provenance and developing using your own/contextual knowledge
- identify the different view of two historians using the content of interpretations
- explain that historians can have two different views about the same event or part of history because of the evidence that they have used to form their view and how they analyse that evidence.
- explain how far you agree with an interpretation of history using another view and your own knowledge.

4 How Hitler became Chancellor, 1932–33

Connect & Engage – Franz von Papen (1879–1969)

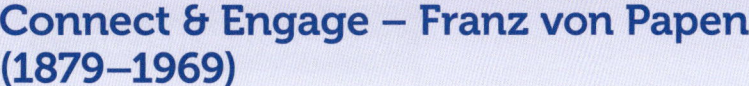

Franz von Papen was born into a Catholic noble family. He served in the Prussian Army from 1898 where he became friends with Kurt von Schleicher. In 1905, he married the daughter of a rich Saarland industrialist which made him very wealthy. Von Papen served as a military expert in the German embassy in the USA during the First World War until he was expelled for spying. He then served as an army adviser to Turkey and ended the war as a lieutenant colonel.

After the First World War, he joined the Catholic Centre Party. He was elected as a deputy in the Prussian State Parliament and was chairman of the conservative newspaper, *Germania*. Von Papen was politically always a supporter of Kaiser Wilhelm II. Von Papen had many connections to wealthy businessmen, the army and to the Catholic Church. He was also an ally and friend of President von Hindenburg.

Chancellor

Despite his limited political experience, von Papen was appointed Chancellor on 1 June 1932. Von Papen's government did not even include any members of the Reichstag and was made up of a group of aristocratic and wealthy men. Von Papen had been a supporter of the earlier presidential government and argued for shutting down the Reichstag altogether. He was forced out of the Chancellor position after he gained little support in the November elections. One of von Hindenburg's advisers, General Kurt von Schleicher, had persuaded von Hindenburg to appoint him as Chancellor over von Papen.

Vice-Chancellor

Von Papen was keen to hold onto his power and influence. He made a deal that Hitler could become Chancellor and von Papen could become Vice-Chancellor. Von Papen was able to persuade a reluctant President von Hindenburg that appointing Hitler as Chancellor was essential to avoiding a civil war in Germany owing to the Nazis having the most seats in the Reichstag. He also convinced von Hindenburg that Hitler would be easy to control if he were Chancellor.

▶ **Source A** Franz von Papen when questioned about whether Hitler would be controllable

You are wrong. We've engaged him ourselves. Within two months we will have pushed Hitler so far into a corner that he'll squeak.

Connect & Engage

1. Read the story of Franz von Papen.
   a. What kind of person was Franz von Papen?
   b. How did von Papen undermine Weimar democracy?
   c. How did von Papen help Hitler become Chancellor?

4.1 How did Hitler become Chancellor of Germany?

Research & Record

Who was responsible for the appointment of Hitler as Chancellor?

You have already read the story of Franz von Papen. Now you are going to find out about the events of 1932 and 1933. Complete the following table on how different individuals enabled Adolf Hitler to become Chancellor in January 1933 as you read pages 58–60.

Individual	How did they damage Weimar democracy?	How did they help Hitler to get into power?
Franz von Papen		
President von Hindenburg		
Kurt von Schleicher		

▶ **Interpretation 1** From *Adolf Hitler*, Ian Kershaw, 1998

At the meeting in August [1932], von Hindenburg refused Hitler the Chancellorship. He could not answer, he said, before God, his conscience and the Fatherland if he handed over the entire power of the government to a single party and one which was so intolerant towards those with different views.

Many factors enabled Hitler to become Chancellor of Germany. We have already looked at some of these:

- The impact of the Great Depression in causing a huge rise in unemployment and economic and social problems.
- The inability of Weimar governments to deal with the problems of the Great Depression.
- How the policies and actions of the Nazis themselves increased their support.

The details on the next page complete the picture by showing how political scheming all led to Hitler becoming Chancellor in 1933. Franz von Papen, Kurt von Schleicher and President von Hindenburg all played important roles in making Hitler Chancellor, even though none of them wanted it to happen.

Party	July 1932	November 1932
Nazis (NSDAP)	230	196
Social Democratic Party (SPD)	133	121
Communist Party (KPD)	89	100
Centre Party (ZP)	75	70
National Party (DNVP)	37	52
People's Party (DVP)	7	11
Democratic Party (DDP)	4	2

▲ Election results for the Reichstag in 1932. Figures show number of seats gained

1 Brüning and Article 48 (1930–32)

In September 1930 the Nazis achieved a breakthrough in terms of election success. They gained 107 seats in the Reichstag and 6.3 million votes. The result took many people in Germany by surprise. The Nazis were now the second largest party in the Reichstag. However, President von Hindenburg did not trust Hitler and refused to give him a government position. Brüning remained as Chancellor but was now reliant on President von Hindenburg using Article 48 of the Weimar Constitution. This allowed him to use emergency powers to make laws without consulting the Reichstag. This weakened Weimar democracy. Brüning also failed to solve the problems of the Great Depression. His plan to give land belonging to bankrupt landowners to peasants angered von Hindenburg. Without the President's support Brüning had little choice but to resign on 30 May 1932. Brüning was replaced as Chancellor by Franz von Papen.

2 July 1932 – the Nazis win 230 seats

Chancellor von Papen had so little support in the Reichstag that he shut it down after only three days and called another election for 31 July 1932. The Nazis won 37 per cent of the votes and 230 seats. They were now the largest party in the Reichstag. Hitler expected this meant that he would become Chancellor, but von Hindenburg continued with von Papen instead. Von Papen had little political experience and was not supported by the leading political parties (the Nazis, Social Democrats or Communists). Therefore, von Papen called another election for November 1932.

3 Von Schleicher becomes Chancellor

The Nazis lost support in the November 1932 election, losing 34 seats and 2 million votes. 'We have suffered a set-back', wrote Joseph Goebbels in his diary. The Social Democratic newspaper *Forwards* proclaimed 'Hitler in Decline'.

Kurt von Schleicher, an army general, brought about the downfall of von Papen's government. Von Schleicher was Minister of Defence in von Papen's government and the two had worked together. However, they fell out in November 1932 after von Papen planned to take power using the military after losing a vote of confidence in the Reichstag. Von Schleicher thought this would lead to civil war and so forced von Papen to resign. In early December 1932, von Hindenburg appointed von Schleicher as Chancellor. Just like von Papen, he struggled to win support for any of his policies. Meanwhile, von Papen was filled with hatred and planned to get revenge against his former ally.

4 Von Papen and Hitler do a secret deal

Franz von Papen began to work with the Nazis. He held a secret meeting with Adolf Hitler where they agreed to form a new government. The agreement said that Hitler would be Chancellor and von Papen would be Vice-Chancellor. Von Papen saw this as an opportunity to get revenge on von Schleicher for what he saw as his betrayal.

5 Hitler becomes Chancellor

With von Schleicher struggling with lack of support, von Papen persuaded von Hindenburg to make Hitler Chancellor. Von Hindenburg never trusted Hitler and was always reluctant but von Papen told von Hindenburg that Hitler could be controlled. Von Papen's plan was for only three Nazis (Hitler and two others) to join a cabinet of 12 to govern Germany. Von Papen's connections meant that his plan had the support of wealthy businessmen, army generals and landowners. They supported the plan as they believed that Hitler and the Nazis would be able to control the Communists. Therefore, on 30 January 1933, von Hindenburg appointed Adolf Hitler as Chancellor of Germany.

Apply ▶ Exam Practice

Question 1 style

Give two things you can infer from Source B about the power of the Hitler and the Nazis before he was appointed Chancellor. **(4 marks)**

> ▶ **Source B** An account by Otto Meissner, State Secretary in von Hindenburg's office, made to the Nuremberg Tribunal after the Second World War
>
> Despite von Papen's persuasions, von Hindenburg was extremely hesitant, until the end of January, to make Hitler Chancellor. He wanted to have von Papen again as Chancellor. Von Papen finally won him over to Hitler with the argument that the representatives of the other right-wing parties which would belong to the government would restrict Hitler's freedom of action. In addition, von Papen expressed his misgivings that, if the present opportunity were missed, a revolt of the national socialists and civil war were likely.

Exam Tip

Making inferences from a source (Question 1)

Look again at the advice on how to approach this type of question on pages 12 and 15.

Remember to:
- identify two inferences from the source
- support each inference with a detail or quotation.

Part 2: Review

> **Revision Tip**
>
> **Test yourself so you are clear on any gaps in your knowledge**
>
> You have now completed half of your GCSE History course. It is important to identify any gaps in your knowledge. You may have missed a lesson or just not fully understood a key concept. One way to identify things you don't know is to regularly test yourself. For Topic 2 think about these questions:
>
> - How did Hitler change the Nazi Party 1920–22?
> - What were the causes and consequences of the Munich Putsch?
> - Why did the Nazis have limited support in the years 1924–29?
> - Why did the Nazis increase their support in the early 1930s?
> - How was Hitler able to become Chancellor in January 1933?
>
> Write out these questions and create a mind map on them using as much as you can remember. Then check your understanding against the information in the book so you can identify things you don't fully remember yet. Do this regularly. The more you retrieve and review information, the better you will remember. After you have checked what you missed out in your mind map, add these details in a different colour – this helps to focus additional revision.

Apply ▶ Recall Challenges

Key individuals

Study these individuals.

- Adolf Hitler
- Anton Drexler
- Gregor Strasser
- Franz von Papen
- Paul von Hindenburg

For each one, try to answer these questions from memory. Get somebody else to test you.

- Who were they?
- What were their aims and beliefs?
- What was their impact and importance?

Key events

Study these key events.

- Munich Putsch
- Bamberg Conference
- Wall Street Crash
- Great Depression
- 1932 Presidential election
- Hitler and von Papen's deal
- Hitler appointed Chancellor

For each event fill in this table to help you recall the details.

What?	When?	Who?	What happened?

Know your key words

Read the following key words and write a definition of each one. Use the glossary to help you remember some of the main words if you get stuck. Get somebody else to test you on the meaning of the key words.

Hitler's rise to power, 1919–33		
25-Point Programme	Putsch	*Mein Kampf*
Article 48	National Socialists	The SA
Propaganda	Coalition	Nationalism
NSDAP	Communism	Freikorps

Apply ▶ Exam Practice

Question 2 style

These exam-style questions test your understanding of Part 2. Practise them now. Use the Exam Tips in the book to help you.

> Explain why Hitler attempted to take power in the Munich Putsch in 1923.
>
> **You may use the following in your answer:**
> - Hyperinflation
> - Nazi support in Bavaria
>
> **You must also use information of your own.** (12 marks)

> Explain why the Nazis had so little support in the years 1924–29.
>
> **You may use the following in your answer:**
> - Gustav Stresemann
> - The Bamberg Conference
>
> **You must also use information of your own.** (12 marks)

> Explain why the Nazis became the most popular political party in Germany by 1932.
>
> **You may use the following in your answer:**
> - Adolf Hitler
> - Propaganda
>
> **You must also use information of your own.** (12 marks)

Summarise

1. Look at the memory aid to help you remember how Hitler became Chancellor.

   Anger at Weimar Republic
   Bankrupt businesses
   Coalition governments
   Deal with von Papen
   Economic problems
   Fear of communism
   Goebbels' propaganda
   Hitler's charisma

   Complete the memory aid (right) that summarises how life changed during the Depression. You may want to use extra visual images and different colours to show political changes and economic changes.

   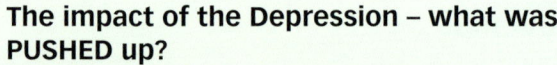

   The impact of the Depression – what was PUSHED up?

   ↑ **P**overty
   Unemployment
   Support for extreme political parties
   Homelessness, crime and violence
   Economic problems
   Dissatisfaction with the Weimar Republic
   What went down?

2. Create your own memory aid that summarises Hitler's path to dictatorship.

1 The creation of a dictatorship, 1933–34

Connect & Engage – Ernst Röhm (1887–1934)

Ernst Röhm was born in Munich, Germany. He joined the German army at the age of 19 in 1906. He was wounded three times in the First World War and received the Iron Cross First Class for bravery. Röhm remained in the army after the war and also supported the Freikorps. He became a close associate of Adolf Hitler when they met through the German Workers' Party in 1919. Röhm used his military connections to set up the SA along with Hitler.

Röhm was involved in the Munich Putsch of November 1923 and was given a suspended prison sentence for his actions. He briefly became a Nazi member of the Reichstag in 1924. Röhm fell out with Hitler in 1925 over the direction of the Nazi Party and resigned. He emigrated to Bolivia and became an adviser to the Bolivian army.

Röhm returns

Röhm returned to Germany and the Nazi Party at Hitler's request in 1930 so he could bring the SA under control. Röhm reorganised the SA and continued its campaign of violence against Jewish people, Communists and opponents of the Nazis. The SA grew greatly under Röhm and became very powerful.

In January 1933, Adolf Hitler became Chancellor of Germany, but he was in a weak position. President von Hindenburg could have dismissed him at any time. Throughout 1933, Röhm supported Hitler with the SA to remove political opponents and establish Hitler's dictatorship.

Röhm's downfall

By 1934, Hitler had come to the realisation that Röhm posed a threat to his power. The SA numbered 3 million. Röhm believed Hitler had abandoned Nazi ideals and sought a 'Second Revolution' which would see the Nazis do more to support the working class.

This led to Hitler purging the SA and killing Röhm on the Night of the Long Knives in June 1934. Röhm's murder was a pivotal moment in Hitler's establishment of his dictatorship and enabled Hitler to win over the support of the German army. Hitler's treatment of his long-term friend shows his ruthlessness in securing a dictatorship.

Connect & Engage

1. Read the story of Ernst Röhm above. What impression do you get of the kind of person he was?
2. Hitler and Röhm had been good friends. Why do you think Hitler needed to remove Ernst Röhm in order to have complete control over Germany?

1.1 Hitler becomes Chancellor

Research & Record

What prevented Hitler having total power when he became Chancellor?

As you read this page, list all the factors that prevented Hitler having total power in Germany when he became Chancellor on 30 January 1933.

Adolf Hitler was appointed Chancellor of Germany on 30 January 1933. However, his position was relatively weak.

As you can see, Franz von Papen and von Hindenburg thought they would be able to control Hitler. However, over the next few months, Hitler set about increasing his power and control through a series of events.

- Germany was still a democracy. The Nazis were the largest party in the Reichstag but only had 196 seats. They did not have the majority they needed to pass the laws they wanted. Sixty-three per cent of voters did not support the Nazis in the November 1932 election.

- There were only three Nazis in the cabinet. They were Adolf Hitler (Chancellor), Wilhelm Frick (Minister of the Interior) and Hermann Göring (no specific role). Franz von Papen was the Vice-Chancellor.

- There were lots of ways in which people could oppose the Nazis. Trade unions represented workers' rights. Political parties such as the Social Democrats and the Communists were well supported.

- President von Hindenburg was the most powerful person in Germany. He had the power to sack Adolf Hitler as Chancellor at any time. The Army was loyal to him.

- Ernst Röhm was the leader of the SA and the 3 million members were personally loyal to him rather than to Adolf Hitler. This meant Hitler did not have full control of the Brownshirts.

- There was freedom of speech and press in Germany, meaning that people could easily oppose the Nazis when they got into power. The law courts were not under the control of the Nazis.

1.2 The Reichstag Fire and its impact

Research & Record

How was Hitler able to create his dictatorship, 1933–34?
As you read through the next six pages, complete your own table like the one below to record the impact of each event on enabling Hitler to create his dictatorship.

A **dictatorship** is a type of government when one person or a group has almost complete power.

Event	What was the impact of each event on Hitler's power?	How important was the event for enabling Hitler to become a dictator?
Hitler becomes Chancellor		
The Reichstag Fire		
The elections of March 1933		
The Enabling Act		
Removing opposition (trade unions, political parties, state governments)		
The Night of the Long Knives		
The death of President von Hindenburg		
Army oath of allegiance		

The Reichstag Fire (February 1933)

On hearing that Hitler had been appointed Chancellor of Germany, Marinus van der Lubbe, a Dutch Communist, travelled to Germany. He had already set fire to three public buildings before setting his sights on the Reichstag on 27 February 1933.

> **Historian Frank McDonough takes up the story …**
>
> 'Security at the building's western entrance was extremely lax. Van der Lubbe nimbly climbed a wall, broke a window and was soon on the first floor of the deserted building. A witness on the street down below, a theology student, heard breaking glass as he walked by and noted the time: 9:30 p.m. Looking up, he saw a person at the window with a burning object in his hand. He ran to alert a policeman. Van der Lubbe, stripped to the waist, dripping with sweat, was quickly apprehended by the police inside the burning Reichstag. It was some time before the fire brigade was alerted, however. The first fire engine did not arrive until 10 p.m. by which time the blaze was completely out of control.'

The Reichstag building was almost totally destroyed. Marinus van der Lubbe was put on trial along with other Communists and executed for the crime on 10 January 1934.

What happened afterwards?

When Hitler heard the Reichstag was on fire he reportedly shouted 'It's the Communists'. Hermann Göring, a leading Nazi, said 'This is the beginning of the communist uprising'.

Historians have often debated whether the Nazis were responsible for the **Reichstag Fire**. What is certain is that the Nazis exploited the fire ruthlessly. Joseph Goebbels spread anti-communist propaganda, and 4000 Communist leaders were arrested. Hitler persuaded President von Hindenburg to use his emergency powers to pass the **Law for the Protection of People and the State** (sometimes known as the Reichstag Fire Decree). This ended freedom of speech and press. It also allowed the government to arrest people without charge. The law was used to attack opponents, especially Communists.

The elections of March 1933

Hitler had already called an election for 5 March 1933 before the Reichstag Fire. He wanted to gain a majority for the Nazi Party. Despite widespread voter intimidation by the SA, arrests of Communists and propaganda, the Nazis failed to win a majority. They polled 43.9 per cent of votes. The election shows the opposition that still existed to the Nazis. However, the Nazis could work with the National Party (a right-wing political party that shared some Nazi ideas such as nationalism) in order to gain a majority in the Reichstag.

The Enabling Act (March 1933)

In order to create a dictatorship, the Nazis needed to change the Weimar Constitution, which meant changing the law. To do this, Hitler needed the support of two-thirds of the Reichstag. Hitler was able to do this firstly by persuading von Hindenburg to use emergency powers to prevent the Communists from taking up their 81 seats in the Reichstag (which was now meeting at the Kroll Opera House). Secondly, he won the support of the National Party who supported Hitler's policies. Thirdly, he persuaded the Centre Party to support him by promising to defend the interests of the Catholic Church. All this gave him the majority he needed to pass the **Enabling Act** by 441 votes to 94.

Party	Seats
Nazis (NSDAP)	288
Social Democratic Party (SPD)	120
Communist Party (KPD)	81
Centre Party (ZP)	74
National Party (DNVP)	52

▲ Reichstag election results – 5 March 1933

The Enabling Act meant Hitler could now pass laws for the next four years without getting the approval of the Reichstag. Article 3 of the Enabling Act said 'the laws passed by the government shall be issued by the Chancellor'.

Banning trade unions (May 1933)

The Enabling Act effectively meant Hitler was able to make whatever laws he wanted. One of his first laws shut down trade unions in May 1933. All trade unions were merged into a new Nazi controlled organisation called the **German Labour Front (DAF)**. This reduced the power of workers to oppose the Nazis by organising strikes.

Banning other political parties (July 1933)

The Communists and the Social Democrats had already been banned by July 1933 but other political parties remained. On 14 July 1933 a law was passed which banned all political parties except the Nazis. This meant that the only legal political party in Germany was the Nazi Party.

1.3 The Night of the Long Knives (June 1934)

The threat of Röhm and the SA

As we have seen in the story of Ernst Röhm, by 1934 the SA were an increasing threat to the power of Adolf Hitler.

The power of the SA
The SA numbered 3 million. Many of them were unemployed, angry and resentful. They were also loyal to Röhm, meaning they could threaten Hitler's power.

The ideas of Ernst Röhm
Röhm did not fully support Hitler and felt he was too close to conservatives, rich businessmen and military generals. Röhm wanted a 'Second Revolution' which would see more socialist policies to support the working class – exactly the kind of people who were in the SA.

The army
The German army was known as the Reichswehr. Many army officers were worried about the power of Röhm and the SA. The SA was much bigger than the Reichswehr, which only numbered 100,000.

The SS
The SS leaders Heinrich Himmler and Reinhard Heydrich resented the power of Röhm. They wanted the SA weakened so they could increase the power of the SS (Blackshirts).

What happened during the Night of the Long Knives?

On 30 June 1934, Hitler ordered Ernst Röhm and 100 other SA leaders to go to a hotel in Bavaria for a meeting. Hitler and a group of SS officers entered the hotel and arrested the SA leadership. Many of them were later killed. On 1 July 1934 Ernst Röhm was given the option to kill himself or be killed. Röhm refused to kill himself and was brutally shot dead by two Nazis.

The consequences of the Night of the Long Knives

Hitler also used the Night of the Long Knives to remove other opponents. Kurt von Schleicher, Gustav von Kahr (from the Munich Putsch) and Erich Klausener (an important Catholic) were killed. Although Franz von Papen, Vice-Chancellor, was not arrested, he was made to resign from the government. Officially, 85 people were killed on the Night of the Long Knives, but the true figure is almost certainly much higher. The SA continued to exist after the Night of the Long Knives but its numbers dropped and it was far less powerful.

The Night of the Long Knives showed the ruthlessness of Hitler and the Nazis. It removed a potential source of opposition in Röhm and the SA. Hitler also won the support of the army and von Hindenburg officially thanked Hitler for his decisive action. It led to the SS growing in power. Meanwhile, Hitler was able to use it to warn his enemies about opposing him as shown in Source B. After the Night of the Long Knives, it was only the ageing President von Hindenburg who stood in his way of fully establishing a dictatorship in Germany.

President von Hindenburg to Adolf Hitler after the Night of the Long Knives

You have saved the German nation from serious danger and for this I express to you my deeply felt gratitude and my sincere appreciation.

Apply ▶ Exam Practice

Question 3a style

Study Sources A and B

How useful are Sources A and B for an enquiry into the consequences of the Night of the Long Knives?

Explain your answer using Sources A and B and your own knowledge of the historical context. (8 marks)

> ▶ **Source A** An extract from Joseph Goebbels' diary, 1 July 1934
>
> Executions nearly finished. A few more are necessary. That is difficult, but necessary... It is difficult, but is not however to be avoided. There must be peace for ten years. The whole afternoon with the Führer. I can't leave him alone. He suffers greatly, but is hard. The death sentences are received with the greatest seriousness. All in all about 60.

> ▶ **Source B** Extracts from Hitler's address to the Reichstag, 13 July 1934, broadcast on the radio
>
> Everyone will know in future that if he lifts his hand against the state certain death is his fate, and every National Socialist [Nazi] will know that no rank and no position allows him to escape punishment.
>
> If anyone reproaches me and asks why I did not resort to the regular courts of justice for conviction of the offenders, then all I can say to him is this: in this hour I was responsible for the fate of the German people, and thereby became the Supreme judge of the German people.

Exam Tip

Evaluating usefulness of sources (Question 3a)

Remind yourself of the CKP advice on page 41 about how to approach this type of question.

C Look carefully at the **content** of the sources. Explain what we can learn from each one about the consequences of the Night of the Long Knives.

K Use your **contextual knowledge**. This source shows/tells us that ... (link content of the source to contextual knowledge). Can you remember the key consequences of the Night of the Long Knives? Review your knowledge before you plan your answer.

P Use the **provenance** of the source. Explain why the nature/author of the source is useful for this enquiry and link to the **content**. For example, in Source B it is Hitler himself speaking. His purpose may be to justify his actions and so it is useful for seeing how Hitler was using the Night of the Long Knives to warn his enemies about opposing him.

1.4 Hitler becomes the Führer

After the Night of the Long Knives, Hitler was almost in complete control of Germany. Nevertheless, he had not fully established his dictatorship.

The death of President von Hindenburg

Paul von Hindenburg died on 2 August 1934 at the age of 86. In preparation for von Hindenburg's death, the Nazis had passed the **Act Concerning the Head of State**. As soon as von Hindenburg died, the power of the President passed to Hitler. On 2 August 1934, von Hindenburg's death enabled Hitler to become the Führer, a title meaning 'leader'. A referendum was held on 19 August 1934. This confirmed Hitler's position as Führer, with 90 per cent of voters supporting Hitler. Many were influenced by propaganda and terror.

The army oath of allegiance

Germany's President was the head of the armed forces. Therefore, when Hitler 'became' Führer he also became Commander in Chief of Germany's armed forces. The army were made to take an oath of allegiance to show their loyalty to Hitler. Hitler had completed his steps to a dictatorship and was now in complete control of Germany.

Apply ▶ Recall Challenge

1. Sequencing. Put these ten events from Hitler's establishment of a dictatorship into the correct chronological order.

The Reichstag Fire	The Nazis win 288 seats in the election
Law for the Protection of People and the State	All other political parties banned
The death of President von Hindenburg	President von Hindenburg appoints Hitler as Chancellor
Trade unions banned	The Night of the Long Knives
Army oath of allegiance	The Enabling Act

2. Revisit your knowledge. What can you recall about these key events from the first part of the GCSE course?

The German Revolution (Nov 1918)	The Spartacist Rising (Jan 1919)
The Treaty of Versailles (June 1919)	The Kapp Putsch (March 1920)
The Munich Putsch (Nov 1923)	The Dawes Plan (August 1924)
The Locarno Treaties (Dec 1925)	The Wall Street Crash (Oct 1929)
The Young Plan (Feb 1929)	The role of Franz von Papen as Chancellor (1932)

Apply — Exam Practice

Question 2 style

Explain why Hitler was able to create a dictatorship in Germany between January 1933 and August 1934.

You may use the following in your answer:
- The Enabling Act
- The Night of the Long Knives

You must also use information of your own. (12 marks)

Summarise

Look at the diagram that shows you the steps that Hitler took to become a dictator of Germany. Make your own diagram to help you remember the 'steps' that Hitler took to become the dictator of Germany.

August 1934 Death of von Hindenburg. Hitler becomes Führer – army take oath of allegiance.

June 1934 Hitler got rid of opposition from within the SA and the Nazi Party in the **Night of the Long Knives.**

Spring and summer 1933 Hitler used the **Enabling Act** to ban trade unions and all other political parties.

24 March 1933 The Enabling Act gave Hitler the power to pass any law without the consent of the Reichstag.

5 March 1933 Elections were held. The Nazis won 288 seats but did not have a majority.

27 February 1933 The Reichstag was set on fire. It was blamed on Dutch Communist Marinus van der Lubbe. The Reichstag Fire Decree reduced the power of the Communists.

30 January 1933 Von Hindenburg appointed Adolf Hitler as Chancellor. There were only two other Nazis in the cabinet of 12.

Exam Tip

Use connectives and evidence for stronger arguments (Question 2)

When explaining why an event/change took place, you have to prove the reason was a cause. For example:

The first reason why Hitler was able to create a dictatorship in Germany was the Enabling Act. **For example**, the Enabling Act was a law that gave Hitler the power to make laws without the Reichstag for four years. **This meant that** Hitler no longer needed support in the Reichstag which immensely reduced its power. He used the Enabling Act to remove trade unions and ban all other political parties.

Use the bullet points in the question

Use the information above to complete two developed explanations using the bullet points in the question (you do not have to use these bullets but it's a good idea as long as you know the details about the event).

1. The first paragraph should prove that the Enabling Act led to Hitler creating a dictatorship. You can base that on what you have learned on this topic. For example, the Enabling Act reduced political opposition.
2. The second should prove that the Night of the Long Knives led to Hitler creating a dictatorship. You can base that on what you learned on this topic. For example, the Night of the Long Knives removed the threat of the SA and gained the support of the army.

Remember to include a third key aspect of content from your own knowledge

The third paragraph could prove that Hitler wasn't able to legally consolidate his dictatorship of Germany until Hindenburg died in August 1934. You can support this with an explanation of how Hitler sized this opportunity to combine the roles of Chancellor and President as Fuhrer and legally consolidate his power.

Use connectives to tie what you know to the question

Phrases like 'this meant that', 'this led to', and 'this resulted in' are called connectives because they tie what you know to the question and so help you prove your argument.

Add specific knowledge

Provide evidence to support your argument. Use phrases such as 'for example', 'such as' and 'this demonstrates' to introduce or flag your supporting evidence.

2 The police state

2.1 How did the Nazis control the German people?

> **Research & Record**
>
> How did the police state enable the Nazis to control people?
>
> Study the information on these three pages.
>
> 1. Create six **category** cards like this to sum up how the police state enabled the Nazis to control people. Make one card for each category.
>   a. The role of the SS
>   b. The Gestapo and Kripo
>   c. The legal system
>   d. Concentration camps
> 2. Think carefully about the impact of each of the examples, the consequences. How did each one enable the Nazis to control people? Produce a **consequences** card for each category.
>
> **CATEGORY CARD** (Identify and describe category)
>
> Led to
>
> **CONSEQUENCE CARD** (Explain consequence)

The Nazis sought to control all aspects of people's lives. This policy was called **gleichschaltung** – it meant bringing everyone in Germany into line with Nazi ideas. A **police state** is when a country has organisations, including the police, that monitor and control people's behaviour, opinions and views. The Nazis sought to remove any kind of opposition including reducing the influence of the Protestant and Catholic Churches within Germany.

The SS (Schutzstaffel)

From 1929, the **SS** was led by **Heinrich Himmler** and by 1933 it had 52,000 members. The SS were obedient and totally committed to Nazism. The SS were supposed to fulfil the Nazi racial ideas of being Aryan. They were expected to have 'racially pure' wives. By 1939, the SS had over 250,000 members.

▲ Heinrich Himmler played a major role in the police state. By 1936, he was in charge of the SS, the SD and the Gestapo

The role of the SS changed after the Night of the Long Knives in June 1934. It became responsible for removing all opposition within Nazi Germany. It had various branches which helped keep order across Nazi Germany.

The Gestapo (Geheimestaatspolizei) and the Kripo

The **Gestapo** was the secret state police. It was set up in 1933 by **Hermann Göring** and was under Himmler's control by 1936. The Gestapo was greatly feared. It arrested and imprisoned anybody suspected of being against the Nazi regime. It had a brutal reputation and could arrest or detain anyone without trial. By 1939, it is estimated that 160,000 people were arrested for political crimes. In reality, the Gestapo only had about 40,000 agents for the whole of Germany and recently historians have questioned the idea that the 'Gestapo were everywhere'. Most Gestapo work was prompted by public informers.

The **Kripo** was the ordinary police responsible for maintaining law and order and dealing with people seen as **asocials** or criminals.

Concentration camps

The Nazis used a type of prison called a concentration camp where opponents were forced to live, without trial. Concentration camps were, at first, used for political opponents of the Nazi regime and were run by the SA, SS and local police forces. The idea was to 'concentrate' opponents of Nazism in one place. The first Nazi concentration camps were set up in old warehouses or factories. Many of these so-called 'wild camps' were closed in mid-1933 and purpose-built camps were made. The first of these was set up at Dachau, outside Munich, in 1933. Other camps followed such as Buchenwald, Mauthausen and Sachsenhausen. The first prisoners were trade unionists, Socialists and Communists. By 1939, there were more than 150,000 people under arrest for supposedly political crimes, showing the extent of opposition to Nazi rule and the control the Nazis had.

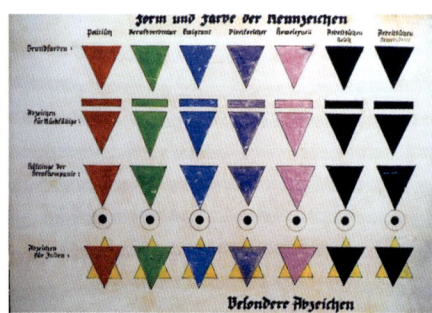

▲ A chart of prisoner markings used at Dachau concentration camp

Prisoners in concentration camps were classified into categories which were signified by a different coloured triangle. Black triangles were for those seen as 'work-shy'. Pink triangles were for gay men. Red triangles were used for political prisoners. Green triangles signified criminals who often worked as 'kapos', who carried out supervisory work of other prisoners. Yellow triangles signified that people were Jewish, while purple was used for Jehovah's Witnesses. Blue denoted foreign forced labour.

Increasingly concentration camp prisoners were forced to work. They worked in quarries, construction sites, coal mines and armament factories. Himmler himself controlled over 150 companies who used this forced labour.

▲ A modern day image of Sachsenhausen. Today the former concentration camp north of Berlin is a museum and memorial

Treatment of prisoners was horrific. Food was scarce and there was abuse, ill-treatment and disease. Many people were released after a short period of time, resulting in German people being aware of the camps and increasing fear of Nazi rule. Some people died in the camps due to the terrible conditions.

The Nazi control of the legal system

The Enabling Act had given Hitler the power to make his own laws. However, he needed to make sure that the law courts and judges interpreted the laws in the way he wanted.

When the Nazis came to power some judges were removed because they were Jewish or had left-wing views. All remaining judges had to join a Nazi organisation called the National Socialist League for the Maintenance of Law (NSRB). In October 1933, the German Lawyers Front was established. Lawyers had to give the Nazi salute and swear 'by the soul of the German people ... to strive as jurists to follow the course of our Führer to the end of our days'. A fair trial was no longer possible in Nazi Germany with the jury system being abolished and trials being conducted by a Nazi judge. Punishments also became harsher. The number of offences which carried the death penalty rose from 3 in 1933 to 46 by 1943.

From 1936, judges had to wear a swastika and Nazi eagle on their robes.

The People's Court

In 1934 the new People's Court was established to try political crimes after Hitler was unhappy with the trial for those accused of being involved in the Reichstag Fire. Roland Freisler was a Nazi judge who was put in charge as the Judge-President. He was known for his ruthlessness. Ninety per cent of cases that came before him ended in a guilty verdict. Between 1934 and 1939, 534 people were sentenced to death for opposing the Nazis. In 1939 alone, there were 150,000 people under arrest for political offences.

▲ Roland Freisler, State Secretary of Reich Ministry of Justice. He is pictured as President-Judge of the People's Court

3 Controlling and influencing attitudes

Connect & Engage – Leni Riefenstahl (1902–2003)

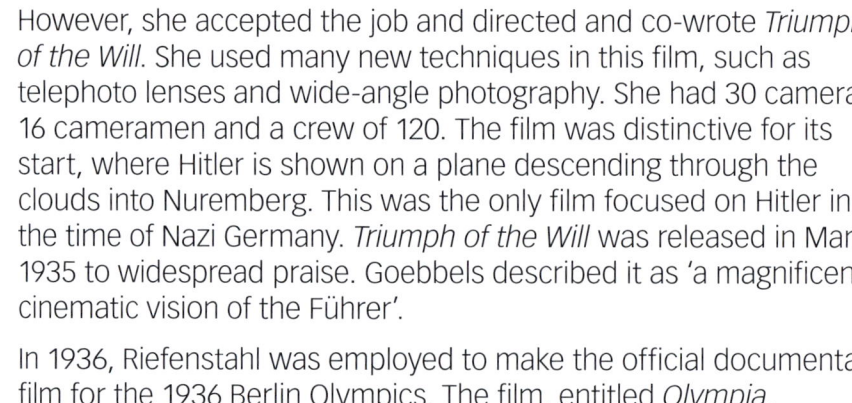

Leni Riefenstahl was born in Berlin on 22 August 1902. She was a talented swimmer, artist and dancer and performed across Europe. In the mid-1920s, she started acting, starring in five films between 1925 and 1929. Riefenstahl was one of a handful of women who directed films during the Weimar era. In 1932, she directed a film called *Das Blaue Licht* (The Blue Light).

In the Nazi era

In 1933, Leni Riefenstahl was hired by Joseph Goebbels to film the 1933 Nuremberg Rally. The resulting film, *Der Sieg des Glaubens* (Victory of the Faith) impressed Hitler, who asked Riefenstahl to make a film about the 1934 Nuremberg Rally. She responded 'I am not a member of the party and I don't even know the difference between the SA and the SS.'

However, she accepted the job and directed and co-wrote *Triumph of the Will*. She used many new techniques in this film, such as telephoto lenses and wide-angle photography. She had 30 cameras, 16 cameramen and a crew of 120. The film was distinctive for its start, where Hitler is shown on a plane descending through the clouds into Nuremberg. This was the only film focused on Hitler in the time of Nazi Germany. *Triumph of the Will* was released in March 1935 to widespread praise. Goebbels described it as 'a magnificent cinematic vision of the Führer'.

In 1936, Riefenstahl was employed to make the official documentary film for the 1936 Berlin Olympics. The film, entitled *Olympia*, premiered in Berlin in 1938.

Triumph of the Will and *Olympia* are widely regarded as two of the most effective and technically innovative propaganda films ever made. However, Riefenstahl's association with Nazi propaganda damaged her career and reputation after the Second World War. After the war, she was arrested but was not charged with war crimes.

Connect & Engage

1. Read the story of Leni Riefenstahl. What impression do you get of the kind of character she was?
2. How did Leni Riefenstahl help the Nazis to control people in Nazi Germany?

3.1 Goebbels and the Ministry of Propaganda

Research & Record

How effective was Nazi propaganda?

Use pages 75–79 to complete your own copy of a table like this. Record example(s) of different types of propaganda. In the third column, write down how effective it was. Complete this once you have finished gathering the evidence.

Use the key sentences on the right to help you to explain how effective the propaganda was.

How effective?
- This was extremely effective
- This was very effective
- This was quite effective
- This was partially effective
- This was not effective

Example of propaganda	Evidence	How effective was it?
Goebbels, propaganda and censorship		
Film		
Rallies		
Sport and the Olympics		
Media (press and radio)		
Propaganda posters		

Joseph Goebbels and the Ministry of Propaganda

In the Nazi rise to power, Joseph Goebbels was in charge of propaganda and in 1933 he became Minister for Propaganda and Popular Enlightenment. The Nazis set up the Ministry of Public Propaganda and Enlightenment and the Reich Chamber of Culture to control the German people and ensure all culture and media put across Nazi views.

> ▶ **Source A** Goebbels explains the purpose of the Propaganda Ministry in *Germania*, a magazine in Nazi Germany, November 1933
>
> In future only those who are members of a Chamber are allowed to be productive in our cultural life. Membership is open only to those who fulfil the entrance conditions. In this way all unwanted and damaging elements have been excluded.

Propaganda means spreading politically biased ideas – e.g. through newspapers, rallies, posters, radio and film.

Censorship is banning things in media, films, books, etc. – in Nazi Germany anything not acceptable to the Nazis was censored.

▲ Joseph Goebbels

Censorship

Alongside propaganda, all media including books, film, newspapers and radio broadcasting was censored by the Ministry of Propaganda. Anything published had to support the Nazis and their ideals. In October 1933, the Nazis passed the Editor's Law to control the content of newspapers. Only positive things could be said or written about the Nazis. Even jokes about the Nazis were censored. People caught saying negative things about the Nazis were sent to concentration camps for 're-education'.

Rallies

The Nazis held huge public meetings of Nazi supporters known as rallies. They involved light shows, marching bands, flags and symbols to create a powerful piece of propaganda. Leading Nazis, including Hitler, would make powerful speeches. The biggest rally was held every year at Nuremberg, usually in late August or September.

Apply ▶ Exam Practice

Question 1 style

Give two things you can infer from Source B about the Nuremberg rallies. (4 marks)

▶ **Source B** William Shirer, an American journalist, describes the Nazi Party rally at Nuremberg in 1934

I got caught in a mob of ten thousand hysterics* who jammed the moat in front of Hitler's hotel, shouting 'We want our Leader.' I was a little shocked at the faces, especially of the women, when Hitler finally appeared on the balcony for a moment … They looked up at him as if he were a Messiah, their faces transformed into something positively inhuman. If he had remained in sight for more than a few moments, I think many of the women would have swooned from excitement.
(* people experiencing uncontrollable emotions)

▲ The Olympic Stadium in Berlin pictured in 2023. The Olympic rings are still there

Sport

The Nazis used sports events as propaganda. They believed an emphasis on sport would develop the focus on fitness for boys to be soldiers and for girls to be healthy and have lots of children.

Visiting international sports teams were required to give the Nazi salute before games. For example, when England beat Germany 6–3 at football in 1938, the players were required to make the Nazi salute. Sporting victories of German athletes were used for propaganda. Max Schmeling was a successful heavyweight boxing champion. He defeated Joe Louis in New York in 1936, although lost a rematch in 1938. His 1936 victory was used to demonstrate Nazi supremacy despite Schmeling not supporting the Nazis. Sports stadiums were covered in Nazi symbols and propaganda posters, further demonstrating how sport was used as propaganda.

The Berlin Olympics (1936)

The Olympics were held in 1936 in Berlin. A new Olympic stadium was constructed on the edges of Berlin which could hold 110,000 people. Hitler wanted the Olympics to demonstrate the superiority of the German people as a 'master race'. Germany headed the medals table with 38 gold medals despite the stand-out performance being the four gold medals won by black American athlete, Jesse Owens.

▲ A poster for the 1936 Olympic Games held in Berlin

Nazi use of media

The Nazis used the media to huge effect. Media includes films (see page 79), the press and radio.

The press

The Nazis passed the Editor's Law in October 1933 which meant that editors would be prosecuted if their newspaper or magazine was not supportive of Nazi ideals. Many non-Nazi newspapers were closed down, with 1400 newspapers being closed by 1935. The Ministry of Propaganda held daily press conferences telling editors what to write. The Nazis also had their own publishing house called *Eher Verlag*. By 1939 they owned 69 per cent of newspapers.

Radio

Radio was a new form of media in the 1930s. The Nazis were quick to realise its power and began to co-ordinate and control the work of the Reich Broadcasting Corporation to ensure all programmes were supportive of Nazi ideas. Goebbels described radio as the 'spiritual weapon of the totalitarian state'. The Nazis mass-produced a cheap radio set as seen in the poster called the Volksempfänger. These could only be tuned to the Nazi radio station so it could not pick up foreign radio stations. By 1939, 70 per cent of households owned one. In addition, loudspeakers in streets made sure that everyone could hear Hitler's speeches when they were being broadcast.

▲ The poster translates as 'All over Germany hear the leader with the people's receiver'. This was a 1936 Nazi Germany propaganda poster featuring a photograph of a crowd of Germans at a Nuremberg Rally surrounding an oversized Volksempfänger radio receiver

▶ **Source C** A newspaper advert, 16 March 1934

Attention! The Führer is speaking on the radio. On Wednesday 21 March, the Führer is speaking on all German stations from 11:00 a.m. to 11:50 a.m. The district Party headquarters has ordered that all factory owners, department stores, offices, shops, inns and blocks of flats put up loudspeakers an hour before the broadcast of the Führer's speech so that the whole work force and all national comrades can participate fully in the broadcast.

▶ **Source D** Philip Gibbs, an English journalist visiting Berlin in 1934

I remember being in a big Berlin café when Hitler was announced to speak over the microphone. The loudspeaker was turned on. Next to me was a group of German businessmen. They went on talking in low voices. At another table was a woman writing a letter. She went on writing. The only man who stood up was a little fellow with his tie creeping over his collar at the back of his head. No one in the crowded café listened to Adolf Hitler.

Apply ▶ Exam Practice

Question 3a style

Study Sources C and D.

How useful are Sources C and D for an enquiry into the Nazi use of the media in 1930s Germany?

Explain your answer, using Sources C and D and your knowledge of the historical context. (8 marks)

Exam Tip

Evaluating usefulness of sources (Question 3a)

Look again at the advice on how to approach this type of question on page 41.

Remember to focus on how the source is useful and to use your knowledge of the focus of this enquiry.

- Make sure you write about the **content** of the sources.
- Use your **contextual knowledge**.
- Write about the **provenance** of the source.

3.2 Nazi control of culture and the arts

Apply ▶ Recall Challenge

Recall your knowledge of Weimar culture. Use pages 34–35 to help you.

1. Answer these recall questions to test your knowledge of Weimar culture.
   a. What was the new style of architecture called during the Weimar Republic?
   b. Which groups were concerned about the new cultural freedoms of the Weimar Republic?
   c. Where was the centre of the world film industry in the Weimar Republic?
   d. Name a famous film produced in Germany during the Weimar Republic.
   e. Give one example of a piece of art that you can remember from the Weimar Republic.
   f. Name one piece of literature you can recall from the Weimar Republic.
   g. What was Neue Sachlichkeit?
   h. Name one piece of theatre you can recall about from the Weimar Republic.
2. Write down five facts you can recall about the story of Magnus Hirschfeld. Read page 30. Then read Interpretation 1 below to find out what happened to him in Nazi Germany.

▶ **Interpretation 1** Frank McDonough tells the story of Magnus Hirschfeld

In Hitler's Germany some individuals became persona non grata (unacceptable) overnight. A typical example was prominent sexual reformer Magnus Hirschfeld, who had championed abortion, sex education in schools, birth control and legalisation of homosexuality in the Weimar years. Hirschfeld was director of the internationally renowned Institute of Sexual Science, which was located in Berlin's affluent Tiergarten district. On 6 May, a number of pro-Nazi students marched into the Institute and vandalised it. Four days later they stole books from its library, which they ceremonially burned in a huge fire nearby. The police did nothing to stop them. Luckily, Hirschfeld was abroad when the raid occurred. He never returned to Germany, dying in Nice on 14 May 1935.

Research & Record

How did culture and the arts change in Nazi Germany?

Using pages 78 and 79 fill in the table to show how culture and the arts changed in Nazi Germany compared with the Weimar Republic.

Cultural form	Weimar Republic	Nazi changes
Art		
Literature		
Architecture		
Film		

The Nazis were against the cultural freedoms of the Weimar Republic. They wanted culture to focus on the glories of Germany's past and to promote traditional family life. The work of Jewish writers, artists and composers would automatically not be part of their new culture.

In September 1933, the Nazis created the **Reich Chamber of Culture** controlled by Joseph Goebbels. Its role was to make sure that all cultural life supported Nazi ideas. This was part of the policy known as **Gleichschaltung**, which meant bringing everyone into line.

Art

Hitler hated modern art and called it 'degenerate'. All working artists had to be members of the Reich Chamber of Culture. Many artists left the country or went into exile. Nazi art was to be clear, direct and portray people as heroic. Hitler himself was portrayed in art as an intelligent and powerful military leader, always dressed in Nazi Party uniform. In 1937 the Exhibition of Great German Art was held in Munich to show off art within Nazi Germany.

Film

The story of Leni Riefenstahl shows you the importance of film for Nazi propaganda. However, only around one-sixth of films in Nazi Germany were made for propaganda. The Reich Film Chamber regulated the content of films. Some films glorified the Nazi rise to power while others taught **antisemitic** ideas. Newsreels were shown before films to give news of the Nazi achievements. The Nazis created a cartoon character called Hansi, the Canary, based on Mickey Mouse. The character resembled Hitler and was sometimes portrayed being attacked by crows which were given stereotypical Jewish features.

Music

Music in the Weimar Republic had been diverse with the cabaret clubs in Berlin. The Nazis created the Reich Chamber of Music which was headed by Richard Strauss. Music by Jewish composers such as Felix Mendelssohn was banned. Hitler's favourite composers such as Richard Wagner, Richard Strauss and Josef Bruckner were all favoured.

Architecture

Hitler described architecture as the 'world in stone'. He favoured architecture based on Greek and Roman architecture, with vast and tall buildings which demonstrated the power of the Nazis. In 1934, the Nazis constructed the Ehrentempel (Honour Temple) as a memorial to the 16 Nazis who died in the Munich Putsch.

For homes, the Nazis favoured a traditional, peasant style of building with pitched roofs and shutters. The Nazis disliked the modern and mass-produced homes that were built during the Weimar Republic.

▲ The Ehrentempel from 1930s Germany

Literature

In May 1933, the Nazis organised the **Burning of the Books** ceremony in Berlin. This was to publicly destroy books that did not support Nazi ideas or were written by those the Nazis did not want to be part of society, such as Jewish people. Around 20,000 books were burnt including Erich Maria Remarque's *All Quiet on the Western Front*, because of its anti-war sentiments.

Instead, the Nazis favoured books that glorified war or peasant rural values, which the Nazis referred to as 'Blood and Soil'. The best-selling book, of course, was Hitler's own work, *Mein Kampf*. People were pressured to own a copy although it is doubtful that many people ever read it.

Albert Speer 1905–81

Albert Speer was born in 1905 and became an architect. He joined the Nazi Party in 1931 and was a key part of Nazi culture. He was central to the 1934 Nuremberg Rally, where he used planes from the German air force to create a dramatic lighting effect. Speer was Hitler's personal architect and drew up plans to rebuild German cities such as Berlin. He was one of the few leading Nazis to be imprisoned after the Second World War.

3.3 How successfully did the Nazis gain control of the Church?

Research & Record

How successfully did the Nazis gain control of the Church?

Read pages 80–82 and gather evidence to support the views in the table.

Interpretation	Support
The Nazis were able to gain control of the Church	The Nazis did gain control of the Church. For example, …
The Church was able to oppose the Nazis	The Church was able to oppose the Nazis. For example, …

The Nazis and Christianity

The historian Michael Burleigh has argued that Nazism was a 'political religion'. The Nazis presented Adolf Hitler as a saviour-type figure and some people in Nazi Germany did seem to 'worship' Hitler in what is known as the 'Cult of the Führer'. There is even a story of some women in Germany eating the gravel that Hitler walked upon.

Around 92 per cent of Germans identified as Christians. With around 40 million Germans belonging to Protestant Churches and 22 million belonging to the Catholic Church, the Churches presented a challenge to the Nazis.

In his rise to power, Hitler avoided attacking the Churches. The Nazis had talked about 'positive Christianity' and religious freedom in their Twenty-Five Point Programme (see page 39). When Hitler came to power, some Christians were sympathetic to some aspects of Nazism. The Churches supported the Nazi focus on traditional family values and its aim to defeat communism. The Catholic Centre Party had supported Hitler to pass the Enabling Act. However, it soon became apparent that the Church and Nazism were not compatible. The Nazis glorified war and violence whereas the Church taught peace, love and respect. The Nazis were cruel to the weak whereas Christian Churches taught that the weak should be supported and cared for.

Exam Tip

Making inferences from a source (Question 1)

You will be asked to make two inferences from a source. To do this successfully, you must look beyond what you can see or what is written in the source and think about what this information suggests. You are looking for what is not shown or said in the source. In your exam, it is important that you use **only the source**, not your own knowledge. For example, when answering this question:

- In the source you can see/you are told that Hitler wants to 'stamp out Christianity in Germany root and branch'.
- From this, we can infer that Hitler sees the Church as a threat and a potential challenge to his own power.

Apply ▶ Exam Practice

Question 1 style

Give two things you can infer from Source A about Hitler's attitude towards the Christian Church. **(4 marks)**

▶ **Source A** Adolf Hitler in a private conversation in 1933

Neither of the denominations – Catholic or Protestant, they are both the same – has any future left. That won't stop me stamping out Christianity in Germany root and branch. One is either a Christian or a German. You can't be both.

The German Faith Movement

Jakob Hauer founded the German Faith Movement in 1934 as a pagan Nazi movement intended to replace Christianity. It encouraged Germans to abandon Christianity and take on pagan rituals instead. It remained fairly small-scale with 200,000 members at its height. This shows that traditional Christian beliefs were still strong.

The Nazis and the Catholic Church

Some Catholics supported the Nazis in the early 1930s because of their anti-communist views. Franz von Papen, who was integral to Hitler coming to power, was himself a Catholic. However, Hitler saw the Catholic Church as a threat. Some Catholic priests did oppose the regime (see page 87) but many did not feel able to.

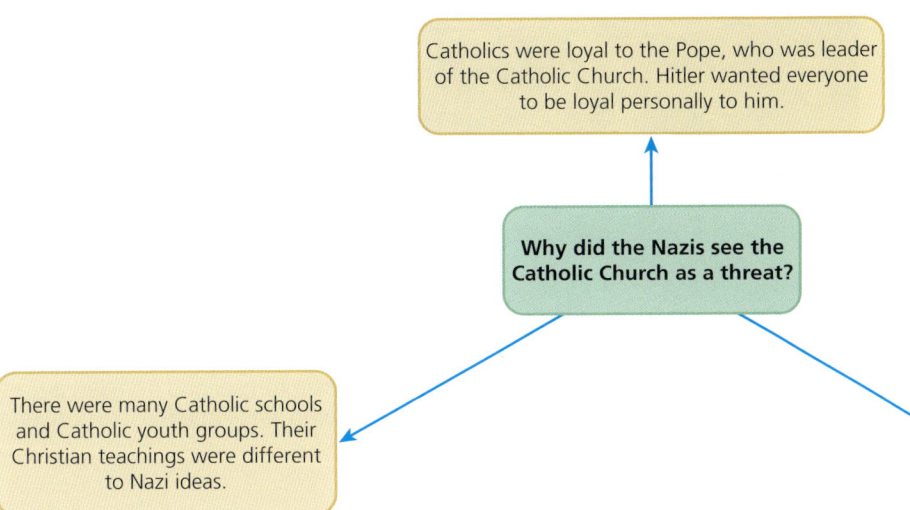

The Concordat (July 1933)

Hitler decided to sign an agreement with the Catholic Church which was known as the **Concordat**. The main features were:

- The Catholic Church would not interfere in politics.
- The Nazis would guarantee religious freedom for members of the Catholic Church.
- The Nazis would not take away the Catholic Church's property or legal rights.
- The Nazis would accept the Catholic Church's control over education and its schools.

At first, relations between the Nazis and the Catholic Church seemed positive as Source B suggests.

The Nazis break the agreement

The Nazis went back on the agreement.

- Many Catholic schools were closed down.
- Youth groups were closed down from 1936.
- A propaganda campaign in 1937 discredited priests, accusing them of sexual abuse.
- Monasteries were accused of sexual and financial misconduct.

▶ **Source B** Public statement by Catholic Bishop Wilhelm Berning, September 1933

The German bishops have long ago said Yes to the new State, and have not only promised to recognise its authority ... but are serving the State with burning love and all our strength.

▶ **Source C** From police reports in Bavaria in 1937 and 1938

The influence of the Catholic Church on the population is so strong that the Nazi spirit cannot penetrate. The local population is ever under the strong influence of the priests. These people prefer to believe what the priests say from the pulpit than the words of the best Nazi speakers.

Apply ▶ Exam Practice

Question 3a

How useful are Sources B and C to an enquiry into relations between the Nazis and the Catholic Church?

Explain your answer, using Sources B and C and your knowledge of the historical context. (8 marks)

- Some priests who opposed the Nazis were arrested and sent to concentration camps.

In 1937, Pope Pius XI issued a sermon to be read out on Palm Sunday, the busiest for attendance at church. The sermon was called 'Mit Brennender Sorge' and meant 'With Burning Anxiety'. This was an open criticism of the Nazi treatment of the Catholic Church and also attacked Nazi racial policies. Also in 1937, a Nazi order banning crucifixes in the classroom was withdrawn after public protests.

These events show that the influence of the Catholic Church remained strong as Source C suggests.

▲ The signing of the Concordat on 20 July 1933. Pictured second from left is Franz von Papen. In the centre is Eugenio Pacelli, who was Pope Pius XII between 1939 and 1958

The Protestant churches

The Reich Church

There were many different Protestant churches within Germany. In 1936, the Nazis sought to unite all the different Protestant churches under the **Reich Church**. Bishop Ludwig Müller, a Nazi, was made Reich Bishop of Germany. Some Protestant churches had the swastika displayed and church services began and ended with the Hitler salute. The Reich Church also attempted to ban the use of the Old Testament of the Bible in services as they said it was Jewish. Although some supported the new Reich Church, many rebelled against it (see page 86).

The Confessional Church

Many Protestants disliked the Nazis trying to take over the Protestant Churches. Some Protestant pastors developed an opposition group called the Confessional Church, which rejected Nazi control of the Church. It was led by Pastor **Martin Niemöller** (see page 84). They set up the Pastors' Emergency League in December 1933 to organise opposition to Hitler. By 1934, it had the support of 7,000 out of 17,000 Protestant pastors.

The Nazis banned the Pastors' Emergency League in 1937 and leaders of the Confessional Church were arrested, reducing the impact and popularity of the Confessional Church. Martin Niemöller was arrested in 1937 and sent to a concentration camp.

▶ **Source D** 1934 Declaration by the Confessional Church

We repudiate the false teaching that there are areas of life in which we belong not to Jesus Christ but to another lord ...

We repudiate the false teaching that the State can and should expand beyond its special responsibility to become the single and total order of human life.

4 Opposition, resistance and conformity

4.1 The extent of support for the Nazi regime

> ▶ **Source A** Franz Noichl was a schoolboy who recalled meeting Adolf Hitler in November 1937 when Hitler visited Sonthofen to inspect one of the Nazis' new Ordensburgen, a type of Nazi fortress
>
> I was eight and remember standing about three metres away from the open car in which Hitler drove by with his arm raised. My father had said goodbye to me with the shocking remark that this would be a good opportunity 'to shoot the criminal'. At the time, I hadn't understood what he meant because everyone else was cheering and praising Hitler – our great leader, who, as the school inspector had explained to us when he visited our class, had ended unemployment and wiped out the disgrace of defeat.

Research & Record

To what extent did German people support the Nazis?

1. Look at Source A. Fill in a table like this. How is each point suggested by the source? This will help you develop your inference skills.

What you can infer	Clues that suggest this in the source
Hitler was a visible leader to the German people.	
Some people did not support the Nazis.	
Some people felt that Hitler was immoral and acted illegally.	
Many people in Germany did support the Nazis.	
Education was used to teach young people to support the Nazis.	
People supported the Nazis as they had solved some of the problems of the Weimar Republic.	

2. Now read the rest of this page and gather evidence to support the views in the table.

Interpretation	Support
German people supported the Nazis in the 1930s.	Evidence that German people supported the Nazis is that …
German people did not support the Nazis in the 1930s.	Evidence that German people did not support the Nazis is that …

President Hindenburg appointed Hitler Chancellor in January 1933, having resisted this in 1932. After being appointed Chancellor, Hitler called new elections for March 1933, gaining 43.9% of the votes.

Many supported the Nazis because they fulfilled their promise of giving people 'Work and Bread'. By 1939, there was no longer any unemployment in Germany.

There was a Cult of the Führer in Nazi Germany with some people almost worshipping Hitler.

There were some groups who opposed the Nazis. For example, there was opposition to the Nazis from **some individuals** within the Church, the army and the young.

There was a high level of people obeying and following Nazi rule. Ninety per cent voted in a referendum to support Hitler becoming Führer in August 1934.

Propaganda and censorship made it difficult to voice opposition. This made it seem to people that the Nazis were popular and well supported.

It is estimated that 300,000 people left Germany in the 1930s due to opposing the Nazis. There were about 1.3 million people sent to concentration camps.

There were three attempts to assassinate Hitler before 1939. The most famous was the attempt by George Elser, who planted a bomb in a Munich Beer Hall in November 1939.

83

▲ A stamp printed in Germany in 1992 commemorating Martin Niemöller

Connect & Engage – Martin Niemöller (1892–1984)

Martin Niemöller was a German nationalist and conservative. He was a U-boat (submarine) commander during the First World War and received the Iron Cross First Class for bravery. He rejected the Weimar Republic and was a battalion commander for the Freikorps against a communist uprising in the Ruhr in 1920.

Niemöller was ordained as a pastor (priest) in 1924. His church was in Berlin when the Nazis came to power in 1933. Like many others in the Protestant Church he welcomed the Nazis because of their anti-communist stance.

Opposing the regime

His views changed and he became a strong opponent of the Nazi regime when Hitler attempted to take control of the Church. Niemöller founded the Pastors' Emergency League in September 1933 to oppose Nazi Church policy. In May 1934, this group issued a declaration of their principles, rejecting any attempt to mix Nazism with the Protestant Church. He co-founded the German Confessional Church in 1934. Niemöller preached sermons which were highly critical of the Nazis.

Niemöller was arrested for speaking out against the Nazis on 1 July 1937. This made headlines around the world but was downplayed in Germany. Goebbels wrote in his diary 'Pastor Niemöller finally arrested … The thing is now to break him, so he can't believe his eyes and ears. We must never let up.' In March 1938, Niemöller was found not guilty of causing a rebellion against Hitler's church policy but found guilty of criticising Hitler. He was sentenced to seven months in prison but was due for release as he had served this time already. However, Hitler ordered for him to be held in 'protective custody'.

Niemöller was held at Sachsenhausen and Dachau concentration camps until the end of the Second World War. He famously wrote a poem which began: 'First they came for the socialists, and I did not speak out because I was not a socialist.' This highlights his belief that silence in the face of injustice only allows it to spread. He realised not standing up to the Nazis endangered everyone. His heroic stance against Nazi oppression resonates with us today and with anyone seeking to stand up to injustice and discrimination.

> 'The Gospel must remain the Gospel; the Church must remain the Church. The creed must remain the creed. Protestant Christianity must remain Protestant Christianity.'
>
> **Martin Niemöller, 19 June 1937**

Connect & Engage

1. What impression do you get from the story about the life and impact of Martin Niemöller?
2. The Church was one of the few groups who were able to oppose the Nazis. Why do you think this was?
3. **Reflect.** The image of Martin Niemöller shows him being commemorated on a German stamp in 1992. Why do you think this happened?

4.2 Opposition and resistance

Research & Record

Which opposition group was the biggest threat to the Nazis?

The police state, propaganda and censorship all made it really difficult to oppose the Nazis. Despite this, some groups did oppose them. Use pages 85–87 to fill in a table like this.

In the final column, think carefully about how big a threat each group was to the Nazis. Award it a threat rating out of five: 5 = the highest threat whereas 0 = no threat.

Who opposed the Nazis?	When? Where?	Why? (Motives)	How? (Methods)	Threat rating (Impact)
Private opposition				
The Church				
Young people				

Private opposition and conformity

Historians have uncovered lots of different examples of opposition to the Nazis from private individuals. Although many people were not actively opposed to the Nazis in terms of organising protests or uprisings, this did not mean they conformed to Nazi rule. Many chose to show non-conformity in what could be seen as 'private opposition'. This opposition was often small-scale but demonstrates that many did not conform to Nazi ideals. Without the coordination of a group, much of this opposition represented very little threat to the Nazis but is still important.

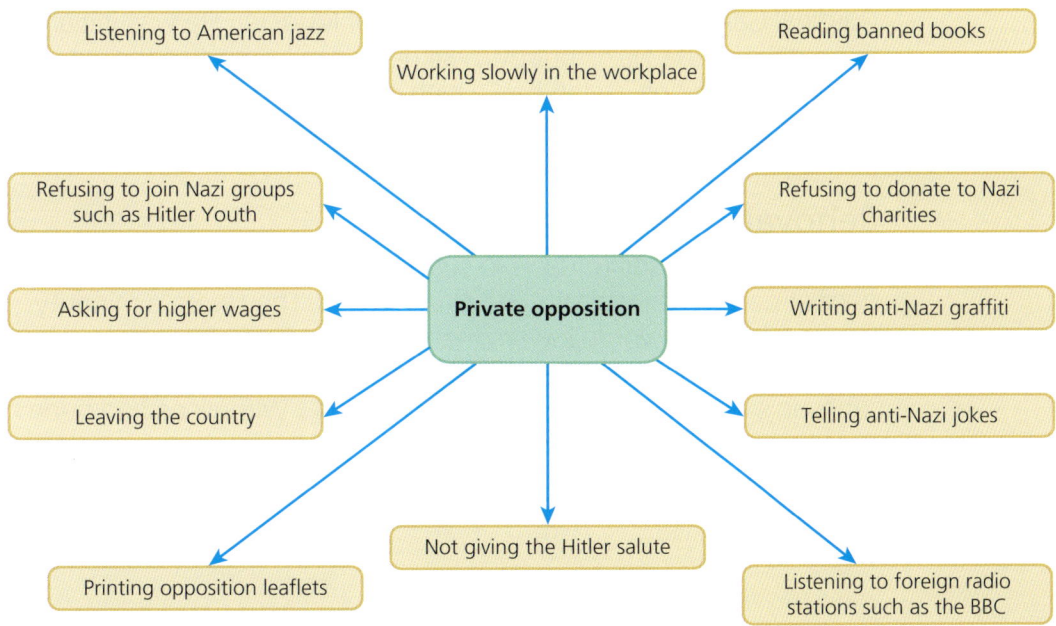

The Church

The Protestant Church

As we have seen, Pastor Martin Niemöller opposed the Nazification of the Church. He became the leader of the **German Confessional Church**. The Confessional Church did not specifically oppose the Nazis but it wanted to keep the Protestant Church free from political control. Niemöller was eventually arrested in 1937 but the fact he was not executed shows he had many supporters and sympathisers, making him a potential greater threat if he was killed.

Dietrich Bonhöffer joined the Confessional Church in 1935. He believed Hitler was hostile to Christianity. He trained pastors and taught them to resist Nazism. This became increasingly difficult throughout the 1930s. In 1938, he joined a resistance group within the German spy network, the Abwehr. He was eventually arrested in 1943 and executed in April 1945.

Paul Schneider was a Protestant pastor who preached against the Nazis in 1933. He was arrested in both 1934 and 1935. He even banned Nazi Party members from attending his services. He was sent to the Buchenwald concentration camp and executed in 1939.

Around 800 of the 17,000 Protestant pastors were arrested but only 50 received lengthy prison sentences for opposition.

The Catholic Church

Despite the Concordat (see page 81) there was conflict after 1933 between the Catholic Church and the Nazis. In 1937, Pope Pius XI issued a special sermon (known as an encyclical) to be read out in all Catholic Churches in Germany on Palm Sunday 1937, which was 21 March 1937. The sermon was known as 'With Burning Anxiety'.

Cardinal Galen was the Catholic Bishop of Münster. He was initially supportive of the Nazis but by 1934 he began to criticise the Nazis within his sermons. Galen had a high profile and was very popular. Although the Gestapo were sent to question him, he was too high profile to remove from power.

Jehovah's Witnesses

Jehovah's Witnesses refused to support the Nazis due to their pacifist beliefs. They wrote anti-Nazi leaflets. They were a minority group, with far fewer followers than the Catholic or Protestant Churches, so the Nazis were more willing to take action against Jehovah's Witnesses. By 1939, 6000 Jehovah's Witnesses had been sent to concentration camps.

Youth Opposition

Hitler said 'Those who have youth on their side, control the future'. Many young people supported the Nazis. However, some of the biggest opponents of the Nazis were young people.

Edelweiss Pirates

The **Edelweiss Pirates** tended to be working-class youngsters. They listened to banned music such as swing music or American jazz. They wore a badge of the edelweiss flower. They also wore clothes the Nazis did not approve of, such as checked shirts. They were more of a movement than an organised group and had different gangs across cities. Some of the names of these gangs were the 'Roving Dudes' from Essen, the 'Kittelbach Pirates' from Dusseldorf and the 'Navajos' in Cologne. They would often meet up to organise their own hikes and camps and sing songs about sex and food. By 1939, membership was estimated to be around 2000. Some groups were politicised and went around beating up Hitler Youth patrols. Despite their opposition, they were not considered a serious threat by the Nazis.

▲ An image of the Edelweiss Pirates, c1938

> ▶ **Source B** An Edelweiss Pirates' song
>
> Hitler's power may lay us low,
> And keep us locked in chains,
> But we will smash the chains one day.
> We'll be free again.
> We've got fists and we can fight
> We've got knives and we'll get them out.
> We want freedom, don't we boys?
> We are the fighting Navajos.

The Swing Youth

The **Swing Youth** were a more middle-class group. They developed mainly in the big cities such as Berlin, Frankfurt and Dresden. They took part in activities that the Nazis did not approve of but were less actively resistant to the Nazis than the Edelweiss Pirates. They took their name from swing music which the Nazis hated. The Nazis classed swing music as being non-German and the music of black people and Jewish people. Swing boys often grew their hair long. The girls often wore make-up and nail polish.

Apply — Exam Practice

Question 3a style

Study Sources C and D. How useful are Sources C and D for an enquiry into opposition to Nazi rule between 1933 and 1939?

Explain your answer, using Sources C and D and your knowledge of the historical context. (8 marks)

Question 3b style

Study Interpretations 1 and 2. They give different views about opposition to Nazi rule between 1933 and 1939.

What is the main difference between these views? Explain your answer, using details from *both* interpretations. (4 marks)

Question 3c style

Suggest one reason why Interpretations 1 and 2 give different views about opposition to Nazi rule between 1933 and 1939.

You *may* use Sources C and D to help explain your answer. (4 marks)

Question 3d style

How far do you agree with Interpretation 2 about opposition to Nazi rule between 1933 and 1939?

Explain your answer, using *both* interpretations and your knowledge of the historical context. (16 marks)

▶ **Source C** SPD member Ludwig Linnert tried to resist the Nazi regime from 1933 until his arrest in 1938. Here he recalls making anti-Nazi leaflets

Justice, freedom and culture – and yes socialism – forced us to warn people and arouse their consciences by distributing illegal leaflets, and writing slogans on the streets, in public squares and on walls.

▶ **Source D** Emmi Bonhöffer, sister-in-law of Deitrich Bonhöffer, interviewed for a 1989 TV programme called *Führer*

There was no resistance movement and there couldn't be. Nowhere in the world can develop a resistance movement when people feel better from day to day. Resistance: we were stones in a torrent (fast flowing water), and the water crashed over us.

▶ **Interpretation 1** Geoff Layton, *Democracy and Nazism: Germany 1918–1945* published in 2019

The underlying trend suggests that the Nazi regime enjoyed increasing popular support from its consolidation during the peace years [1933–1939] … The regime enjoyed a trend of consensus that was not realistically threatened.

▶ **Interpretation 2** J. Hiden, *Republican and Fascist Germany*, 1996

The persecution of hundreds of thousands of Germans by the Hitler regime serves to illustrate that the dissent and nonconformity must have been widespread. Resistance, defined as an organised and sustained attempt to destroy the government, was not widespread.

Exam Tip

Analysing sources and interpretations (Questions 3a, b, c, d)

Look again at the advice on how to approach these types of questions on pages 28 and 29.

Remember to

- explain how each source is useful considering their content, provenance and developing using your own/contextual knowledge
- identify the difference in view of two historians using the content of interpretations
- explain that historians can have two different views about the same event or aspect of history because of the evidence that they have used to form their view, the emphasis they have taken or due to their perspective
- explain how far you agree with Interpretation 2 using Interpretation 1 and your own knowledge.

Part 3: Review

Apply ▶ Recall Challenges

Key individuals

Study these individuals.

- Adolf Hitler
- Martin Niemöller
- Marinus van der Lubbe
- Ernst Röhm
- Leni Riefenstahl
- Joseph Goebbels
- Albert Speer
- Heinrich Himmler
- Dietrich Bonhöffer
- President von Hindenburg

For each one, try to answer these questions from memory. Get somebody else to test you.
- Who were they?
- What were their aims and beliefs?
- What was their impact and importance?

Key events

Study these key events.

- The Reichstag Fire
- The Enabling Act
- Night of the Long Knives
- The Berlin Olympics
- The Burning of the Books
- Death of President von Hindenburg

For each event fill in this table to help you recall the details.

What?	When?	Who?	What happened?	Why was it important?

Know your key words

Read the following key words and write a definition of each one. Use the glossary to help you remember some of the main words if you get stuck. Get somebody else to test you on the meaning of the key words.

Nazi control and dictatorship, 1933–39			
Dictatorship	Gleichschaltung	Propaganda	Censorship
Rallies	Trade unions	Swing Youth	Edelweiss Pirates
Confessional Church	Concordat	Encyclical	Culture
Reich Church	Gestapo	SS	Swing Youth
SA	Concentration camp	Police state	Media

Apply ▶ Exam Practice

Question 2 style

These exam-style questions test your understanding of Part 3. Practise them now. Use the Revision Tip below to help you. Remember that in the exam you will have a choice of two questions for Question 2.

> Explain why Hitler was able to create a dictatorship in the period February 1933 to August 1934.
>
> **You may use the following in your answer:**
> - Reichstag Fire
> - Death of Hindenburg
>
> **You must also use information of your own.** (12 marks)

> Explain why there was little opposition to Nazi rule between 1933 and 1939.
>
> **You may use the following in your answer:**
> - The police state
> - Propaganda
>
> **You must also use information of your own.** (12 marks)

> Explain why the Nazis were able to control the German people in the years 1933–39.
>
> **You may use the following in your answer:**
> - the Reich Church
> - Goebbels and the Ministry of Propaganda
>
> **You must also use information of your own.** (12 marks)

Revision Tip

Complete practice exam questions to test your understanding

Completing regular practice exam questions will help you to hone your skills. You can have a look through some of the exam questions in this book or get them from the exam board website.

Remember to use the **3Ds** to help you when tackling exam questions. Here is an example of how to use this approach for Question 2, which is the 'explain why' question worth 12 marks.

Decode the question and work out the focus of the question.

- Note any dates and make sure you stay focused on the correct time period. You will not get marks if you write outside date boundaries.
- Underline key parts of the question including command words.
- Note the two bullet points which you can use as part of your answer.

Decide how to organise your answer. **This question is worth 12 marks so plan it out carefully.**

- Plan your answer using three paragraphs. Aim to write one paragraph on each of the bullet points.
- You need to go beyond the two bullet points and use three aspects of knowledge.

Develop your answer. **You need to develop the points you make. Lists are not good enough.**

- Don't just write what you know but make sure you link what you say to why an event happened. Use a phrase such as 'this meant that' or 'this led to' to help you to do this.

1 Nazi policies towards women

1.1 Nazi views on women and the family

Apply ▶ Recall Challenge

Before finding out about Nazi policies towards women, review your knowledge of life for women in the Weimar Republic on pages 32 and 33.

Create mind maps with evidence to support both arguments below.
1. The lives of women improved during the Weimar Republic
2. The lives of women did not improve during the Weimar Republic

Research & Record

What were the Nazi aims for women and the family?

Read the information on pages 91 and 92 and make a list of ten key bullet points which summarise the Nazi aims for women and the family. We have done the first two for you.
- Increase the birth rate
- Increase the number of marriages

Women had many freedoms during the Weimar years, including the right to vote and to better career opportunities. The Nazis had very different views on women and the family, as shown in Sources A and B.

▶ **Source B** From a booklet produced by the Reich Committee for Public Health, 1935

1. Remember that you are German.
2. If you are genetically healthy, you should not remain unmarried.
3. Keep your body pure.
4. You should keep your mind and spirit pure.
5. As a German, choose a spouse of the same blood.
6. When choosing a spouse, ask about their forebears (ancestors).
7. Health is also a prerequisite (requirement) for physical beauty.
8. Marry only for love.
9. For a spouse seek a companion, rather than a lover.
10. You should have as many children as possible.

▶ **Source A** Gertrud Scholtz-Klink, Head of the Nazi Women's Organisation

Woman is entrusted in the life of the nation with a great task, the care of man, soul, body and mind. It is the mission of woman to minister in the home and in her profession to the needs of life from the first to the last moment of man's existence. Her mission in marriage is … comrade, helper and womanly complement of man – this is the right of woman in the New Germany.

Women should have lots of children.

More people should get married.

Married women should not work. Instead, they should focus on bringing up children and looking after the home.

The ideal family is Aryan with blonde hair and blue eyes. Women should marry Aryan men to produce racially pure children.

The ideal German family was a peasant family.

Education should teach girls how to be mothers in the future.

▲ A painting by Wolfgang Willrich created in 1938. It shows the ideal German family. Willrich was instructed to portray four children. Willrich was also a member of the SS

Women should dress simply and follow a healthy lifestyle.

The Nazi slogan for women was Kinder, Kirche, Küche meaning Children, Church, Kitchen.

1.2 Nazi policies towards women

Research & Record

What were the Nazi policies towards women?

Read the information on pages 93 to 95.

1. Create three category cards to summarise Nazi policies towards women. Make one card for each of the following categories.
   - Marriage and family
   - Employment
   - Appearance
2. Think carefully about the consequences of the policies for each category. Make a consequences card for each category.

CATEGORY CARD
MARRIAGE AND FAMILY – Marriage loans were introduced to encourage couples to get married.

Led to

CONSEQUENCE CARD
The number of marriages increased slightly and peaked in 1934.

Marriage and family

The Nazi policies on marriage and family aimed to increase the population of strong, racially pure Aryans. They thought that more Aryans would make Germany bigger and more powerful.

Encouraging marriage

In 1933, marriage loans were introduced to encourage couples to get married. Once couples were married, they would have to pay back less money if they had more children. If they had four children, they would not have to pay the loan back at all. The loans were worth about half a year's pay but women had to give up work to qualify for one. Marriages did increase at first to a peak in 1934 but remained fairly consistent.

Divorce was made easier for those marriages that did not produce children. The 1938 Marriage Law allowed a divorce if either the husband or wife did not want to have children or was unable to have children. This led to a big increase in the divorce rate in 1939.

Reasons for divorce	1938–41
Matrimonial offences, including adultery	197,000
Irretrievable breakdown	31,000
Refusal to procreate (have children)	1,771
Infertility	383

▲ Divorce statistics after the 1938 Marriage Law

Increasing the birth rate

The Nazis used propaganda to encourage the birth of more healthy Aryan children. The Honour Cross of the German Mother was a medal given to couples for having lots of children. People with four or five children got a bronze medal, people with six children got a silver medal and people with eight or more children got a gold medal. The medals were given out on 12 August, which had been Hitler's mother's birthday. The Nazis even had a slogan of 'I have donated a child to the Führer'.

Abortion and birth control were restricted. However, some people were not allowed to have children. From 1933 the Nazis forced women and men with inherited diseases or conditions such as colour-blindness to be sterilised. Over 350,000 people were sterilised in Nazi Germany as a result of the policy.

The birth rate did increase slightly, reaching a peak in 1939. The average number of children per couple in 1932 was 3.6 but by 1939 it was 3.3. Historians are divided on how much this was to do with Nazi policies and how much it was to do with other factors such as the improving economy.

Indoctrinating women into Nazi ideals

The Nazis sought to change the role of women around Kinder, Kirche, Küche (Children, Church, Kitchen). The German Women's Enterprise organised classes about motherhood and family life. By 1939, 3.5 million women had attended these classes.

▲ Marriages and live births in Germany 1932–39

Lebensborn

The Lebensborn (spring of life) was founded by Heinrich Himmler and overseen by the SS from 1935. It began as providing homes for unmarried Aryan mothers. Ten homes were created providing maternity facilities. Later on, the Lebensborn homes were used to arrange for women to be impregnated by members of the SS. It is estimated that by the end of Nazi rule, 11,000 children were born as a result of them.

Review and Revise

Statistics can sometimes be difficult to understand. However, historians agree the following about marriage and the family:
- The birth rate did increase after 1933, reaching a peak in 1939.
- The divorce rate increased.
- The number of marriages was fairly consistent.

Employment

The Nazis did not count women in their unemployment statistics and they encouraged married women not to work through propaganda. This helped the Nazis to achieve their promise of 'Work and Bread'.

As well as discouraging women from applying for jobs and companies from hiring them, women were banned from some professions. In 1933, female doctors and women in the civil service lost their jobs, followed by female judges and lawyers in 1936.

Women were also discouraged from going into higher education. The number of women going to university went down to 10 per cent.

Did the number of women working decrease?

At first, the number of women in jobs fell. The percentage of women in employment went from 37 per cent to 31 per cent between 1932 and 1937.

However, when Germany began to rearm after 1936, the Nazis had to reverse their policy on women and employment. They needed more people, including women, to work. They reduced the marriage loans scheme. As a result, more women worked overall and there were more women in every type of job, as can be seen in the table below.

Despite this, by 1939 Germany was still suffering from a labour shortage.

Job	1933	1939
Agriculture and forestry	4.6	4.9
Industry and crafts	2.7	3.3
Trade and transport	1.9	2.1
Non-domestic services	0.9	1.1
Domestic service	1.2	1.3
Total	11.3	12.7

▲ Women's employment (in millions)

Appearance

The Nazis promoted a healthy lifestyle for women so they could give birth to many children. Exercise was encouraged while smoking, being too slim or going out for late nights was discouraged. The Nazis wanted women to style themselves on a traditional peasant look. Women were not supposed to wear trousers, short skirts or high heels. Wearing make-up and dyeing or styling hair was also frowned upon.

Many women rebelled against Nazi ideals. The cosmetics industry, however, began creating new products to help women achieve this natural, peasant look.

Many wives of leading Nazis ignored the Nazi ideal on women's appearance. Magda Goebbels, who was married to Joseph, was often photographed smoking in public. Emmy Göring, wife of Hermann, showed off her Paris fashions and cosmetics. The Görings often hosted lavish parties including a famous moonlit ball during the 1936 Olympics.

Apply ▶ Exam Practice

Question 3a style

How useful are Sources C and D for an enquiry into Nazi views towards women?

Explain your answer, using Sources C and D and your knowledge of the historical context. (8 marks)

▶ **Source C** *The Farming Family from Kalenberg* by Adolf Wissel, 1938. Hitler himself bought this painting in 1939

▶ **Source D** A speech made by Joseph Goebbels, 1939

The mission of women is to be beautiful and bring children into the world … The female bird pretties herself for her mate and hatches eggs for him. In exchange, the mate takes care of gathering the food, and stands guard and wards off the enemy.

Exam Tip

Evaluating usefulness of sources (Question 3a)

Look carefully at the **content** of the sources. Explain what we can learn from the source about Nazi views towards women.

Top tip: When analysing images make sure you go beyond describing the image to explaining what you can infer about a source and why this would be useful.

For example, from Source C I can infer that the Nazi view towards women is that their role was a mother. I can tell this because the woman is shown cuddling her child which implies that it is important for women to look after their children. This would be useful as a historian can clearly see how women were being portrayed by the Nazis.

Use your **contextual knowledge**. How does the source link to your knowledge of the topic?

Use the **provenance** of the source. Explain why the author of the source is useful for this enquiry.

For example, Source C is a propaganda image of a peasant family produced in 1939. The artist would have produced this source to persuade women and families to follow Nazi ideals. This is useful for showing how the Nazis put across their views towards women.

2 Nazi policies towards the young

Connect & Engage – Baldur von Schirach (1907–74)

Baldur von Schirach's father was an officer in the German army and his mother was American. He joined the Nazi Party in 1924 and by 1931, he was a Nazi Youth Leader. In 1933 he became the leader of the **Hitler Youth**. The Hitler Youth was a youth group for boys and girls in Nazi Germany that promoted Nazi ideals.

His main role was to ensure young people joined. Years later, he described his task as making German youth believe 'that Hitler created the world in six days, with the seventh set aside for making Hitler Youth parades'. His main challenge was replacing the already strong and popular Roman Catholic youth movement.

Baldur von Schirach featured greatly in propaganda in Nazi Germany. As a favourite of Hitler, he stood for everything the Nazis thought was good about Germany. He even wrote poems to Hitler. Some other leading Nazis did not like what they saw as his effeminate nature.

In 1940, he became Gauleiter (governor) of Vienna in Austria and supervised the deportation of Jewish people. Later on he denied any knowledge of the Holocaust. He was sentenced to 20 years in prison after the Second World War and was released in 1966. In later life, he often tried to downplay his role as a leading Nazi.

Connect & Engage – Trude Mohr (1902–89)

Trude Mohr's family were nationalists. She joined the German nationalist movement in the 1920s and became a **League of German Maidens** (Bund Deutscher Mädel – BDM) leader. This was a Nazi youth movement for girls. She became the overall leader of the League of German Maidens in 1934. Her role was to instil girls with Nazi ideas and prepare them for their future roles as wives and mothers.

In 1937, she stepped down after marrying an SS officer and becoming pregnant. Her organisation had grown to 2.7 million members. She was succeeded by Jutta Rüttiger.

After the Second World War, she was briefly captured by the British but released and continued to live in Germany.

Connect & Engage

Read the stories of Baldur von Schirach and Trude Mohr.

1. Why do you think the Nazis put so much emphasis on influencing young people?
2. Can you connect these stories to any of your learning about the Churches and the Nazis' ideas of the role of women?

2.1 Nazi aims towards the young

Research & Record

What were the Nazi aims towards young people?

Read the stories again on page 97 and the collection of sources on this page.

Make a mind map of the main aims the Nazis had towards young people using the information in the sources.

Apply Recall Challenge

Complete the five quiz questions. This knowledge will provide a good foundation for understanding the Nazis and young people.

1. What were the Nazi aims towards women?
2. How did the Swing Movement oppose the Nazis?
3. How did the Edelweiss Pirates oppose the Nazis?
4. What were Hitler's main ideas in *Mein Kampf*?
5. Give an example of how the Nazis used propaganda to influence people.

The Nazis had the following aims for the young:
- Ensure young people had respect for Adolf Hitler.
- Ensure young boys were fit, healthy and tough so they could fight as soldiers.
- Ensure young girls could look after the home and raise healthy, Aryan children.
- Young people should have pride in their country and should be willing to devote themselves to Germany.
- Young people should believe in Nazi ideas.

▶ **Source B** From a speech by Adolf Hitler in 1934

In my great educative work I am beginning with the young. We older ones are used up. We are rotten to the marrow. But my magnificent youngsters! Are there finer ones in the world? With them I can make a new world.

▶ **Source A** Robert Ley, leader of the German Labour Front (DAF)

We start our work when the child is three. As soon as it begins to think, a little flag is put into its hand. Then comes school, the Hitler Youth Movement, the Storm Troop. We never let a single soul go.

▶ **Source C** A poster encouraging girls to join the League of German Maidens (BDM), 1936

2.2 Nazi policies towards the young

Research & Record

Did the Hitler Youth succeed in winning over young people?

Read pages 99 and 100. Gather evidence to support the arguments in the table. You will be able to use these notes to answer the exam question on page 102.

Argument	Support
The Hitler Youth succeeded in winning over young people.	In some ways the Hitler Youth did succeed in winning over young people. For example, the membership figures of the Hitler Youth show that …
The Hitler Youth did not succeed in winning over young people.	In some ways the Hitler Youth did not succeed in winning over young people. For example, the evidence of youth opposition groups suggests that …

Connect & Engage

Begin by **connecting** your learning to the youth opposition groups such as the Edelweiss Pirates and the Swing Movement.

How can you use this information to answer the question: Did the Hitler Youth succeed in winning over young people?

The Hitler Youth

There were many youth groups in Germany before the Nazis came to power. In 1933, the Hitler Youth made up just 1 per cent of youth groups. Within the Hitler Youth there were separate groups for boys and girls at different ages. The membership of the Hitler Youth grew from just 200,000 (1932) to 7.1 million (1938). By 1939, membership of the Hitler Youth was compulsory. All other youth groups had been banned.

Members of the Hitler Youth had to swear an oath of loyalty to Hitler and were taught Nazi ideas. All groups focused on **indoctrination** (teaching people to believe something), **patriotism** (being proud of your country), physical activity and camping trips. However, some of the activities for boys and girls within the groups were very different. This was to prepare them for their future roles in Nazi Germany.

Age group	Organisation
Boys 10–14 years old	German Young People (Deutsche Jungvolk)
Boys 14–18 years old	Hitler Youth (Hitlerjugend)
Girls 10–14 years old	League of Young Girls (Jungmädel)
Girls 14–18 years old	League of German Maidens (Bund Deutscher Mädel, BDM)

▲ The term 'Hitler Youth' also covers the whole range of youth groups under its leader Baldur von Schirach

▲ Adolf Hitler meets with boys of the Hitlerjugend (Hitler Youth), Obersalzberg, Bavaria, c1937

The Hitler Youth and the League of German Maidens

Boys' groups engaged in endless physical and military activities such as marching, map-reading and signalling. They were trained to be strong and fearless – to be the future soldiers and workers of Nazi Germany. Boys took part in even more military training in the Hitlerjugend where there were even military divisions and special training in handling weapons and combat.

Girls were prepared for their future roles as wives and mothers. Activities developed domestic skills such as cooking, sewing and how to look after children.

All groups were taught Nazi racist ideas and the importance of marrying Aryans and having Aryan children.

How popular were the youth groups?

Many young people enjoyed some parts of the Hitler Youth. The mountain camps (see Interpretation 1) were popular and enabled working-class children to leave the city and see the countryside. Some (see Source D) commented how much they enjoyed it at first. By 1939, 80 per cent of young people were members of the Hitler Youth.

By the late 1930s the youth groups were more difficult to run. The increased emphasis on military drill and discipline as Germany prepared for war was unpopular. Many Hitler Youth leaders seemed out of touch. Some young people never joined the Hitler Youth despite it being compulsory. The Nazis had to set up a section of the secret police to monitor young people and a youth concentration camp was created at Neuwied. Opposition youth groups like the Edelweiss Pirates and the Swing Movement show that not all young people were won over by Nazi ideals.

▶ **Interpretation 1** Julia Davis, *A Village in the Third Reich*, published in 2022

Oberstdorf* hosted its own mountain camp organised by the local Hitler Youth and the public welfare department. Two and a half thousand boys from the Chemnitz area (300 miles away in east Germany) stayed in the mountains for two weeks. They set up their own telephone line and post office and built a well, a trough with fresh spring water for washing, and a latrine they nicknamed the League of Nations.

*Oberstdorf was a village set in the mountains of southern Germany on the border with Austria.

▶ **Source D** Arno Klönne remembers his time in the Hitler Youth in a book he wrote in 1982

What I liked about the Hitler Youth was the comradeship. I was full of enthusiasm … what boy isn't fired by high ideals such as comradeship, loyalty, honour, the trips off into the countryside.

Later when I became a leader the negative aspects became obvious. I found the compulsion and the requirement of absolute obedience unpleasant.

2.3 Nazi control of the young through education

Research & Record

How did the Nazis use education to achieve their aims towards young people?

Read this page. Fill in your own copy of this table to find evidence of how the Nazis used education to achieve their aims.

Aim	How education was used to achieve this
Loyalty towards Hitler and the Nazis	
Support of Hitler's racist policies	
Preparing boys and girls for their future roles	
Creating future Nazi leaders	

All children attended school in Nazi Germany from the age of 6 to 14. The Nazis controlled schools through the Ministry of Education. Boys and girls followed a different curriculum and the Nazis preferred separate schools for boys and girls.

Schoolteachers
Schoolteachers had to join the Nazi Teachers' League. By 1937, 97 per cent of teachers had joined and teachers had to show loyalty to Nazi ideas in the classroom.

Lessons
Lessons began with the Nazi salute. Classrooms were covered in images of Hitler and swastika flags. Textbooks were rewritten to fit in with Nazi ideals. *Mein Kampf* was widely studied.

Geography
In Geography, children learned about lands in the East that the Nazis felt should be part of Germany and the amount of land taken away from Germany by the Treaty of Versailles.

Napola and Adolf Hitler Schools
The Nazis set up Napola schools for boys who were singled out for having leadership potential. Adolf Hitler Schools were set up for the young leaders of the Hitler Youth.

Maths
Children were given questions that had political meaning, as you can see in Source F.

Other subjects
Girls learned needlework and cookery to prepare them for their futures. New studies such as Race Studies taught Nazi ideas on race. Religious Education was scrapped.

Physical Education
The amount of PE that children did was increased, with around 15 per cent of curriculum time being spent on it. This was to ensure children were physically fit.

Science
Children learned about the science of the Aryan race in Biology. In Physics lessons, they learned about explosives and weapons of war.

▶ **Source E** Extracts from a Nazi mathematics textbook

Question 95 The construction of a lunatic asylum [a type of hospital for people with mental illnesses] costs 6 million RM (Reichsmarks). How many houses at 15,000 RM each could have been built for that amount?

▶ **Source F** Dr Schuster, a geography teacher describes education in 1938

My headmaster, who is new and young and a very keen Nazi – in fact he would not have the post at all if he were not a Party man – greatly hopes that I will leave. That is obvious, for he will get high praise if he can quickly establish an all-Nazi staff.

Exam Tip

Reaching a judgement (Question 3d)

In the exam, you must reach a judgement about how far you agree with the view in Interpretation 2. The best answers will have an argument and their overall judgement running throughout the answer. For example, when answering the question:

- Plan before you start writing so that you know what your argument and overall judgement will be.
- Decide whether you agree or disagree that young people did not support the Nazis and refer to this in all your paragraphs.
- Return to your argument and overall judgement in your conclusion. Explain why you have reached this judgement by saying, for example, 'In the final analysis, I strongly agree with Interpretation 2 due to the existence of rebel youth groups like the Edelweiss Pirates.'

Apply ▶ Exam Practice

Question 3b style

Study Interpretations 1 and 2.
They give different views about how much young people supported the Nazis.
What is the main different between these views?
Explain your answer, using details from *both* interpretations. (4 marks)

Question 3c style

Suggest **one** reason why Interpretations 1 and 2 give different views about how much young people supported the Nazis.

You may use Sources D (page 100) and F (page 101) to help explain your answer. (4 marks)

Question 3d style

How far do you agree with Interpretation 2 about how much young people supported the Nazis?
Explain your answer, using *both* interpretations and your knowledge of the historical context. (16 marks)

> ▶ **Interpretation 1** Geoff Layton, Democracy and Nazism: Germany 1918–1945, 2019
>
> In some respects, the emphasis on teamwork and extracurricular activities was welcomed by many youngsters, especially when compared to the practice in other European countries. The provision for sports, camping and music genuinely excited many of the youth and for those from poorer backgrounds the Hitler Youth really offered opportunities. Most significantly, the Hitler Youth successfully created an atmosphere of fun and a sense of belonging to the new Germany.

> ▶ **Interpretation 2** Richard Kennett, *Living under Nazi Rule*, 2017
>
> Not every child was so convinced by Nazi propaganda in schools and in the Hitler Youth. Many were bored or resentful at the meetings, especially those who usually avoided physical activity. Others enjoyed parts of the programme but resisted the political message. Some just hated being forced to attend.

Exam Tip

Explaining the difference in views of historians (Question 3c)

You will be asked to explain one reason why two historians have different views about the same event or aspect of history. Consider the evidence they have used to form their view, what they have chosen to emphasise or the perspective they have taken. Do not consider when their views were written. Both interpretations will be from recent publications. In your exam, it is important that you support your reason with quotations from both interpretations. For example, when answering this question:

- Identify that the two views of historians are different because they have a different emphasis.
- Develop and support your answer by proving that Interpretation 1 focuses on the new opportunities that the Hitler Youth offered, such as camps, whereas Interpretation 2 focuses on the fact that the Hitler Youth tried to politically indoctrinate young people.

3 Employment and living standards

3.1 Nazi policies to reduce unemployment

Research & Record

How did the Nazis reduce unemployment between 1933 and 1939?

Use pages 103 and 104 to research the ways in which the Nazis reduced unemployment between 1933 and 1939.

Method	Explanation: How did it enable the Nazis to reduce unemployment?	Evaluation: How important was this in reducing unemployment?
National Labour Service		
Autobahns and public works schemes		
Rearmament		
Invisible unemployment		

Apply ▶ Recall Challenge

Review your knowledge of the economy and living standards in the Weimar Republic. This is important foundational knowledge for this topic.

Match the correct answer with the question.

How many banks went bust in the banking crisis of 1931?	230
In which year was the Wall Street Crash?	6 million
How many seats did the Nazis win in the 1928 election?	5
How many German people were registered as unemployed in 1932?	12
Which article of the Weimar Constitution was used by Brüning to pass emergency laws as Chancellor?	1929
In which year was the hyperinflation crisis?	48
How many seats did the Nazis win in the July 1932 election?	1923

Once in power, the key economic aim for Hitler was to reduce unemployment and create jobs for German workers.

National Labour Service (RAD)

The National Labour Service employed 19–25-year-old men. It began in 1933 but became compulsory in 1935 when all men of this age had to spend six months in the National Labour Service. The work was mostly in agriculture or on public works schemes (see below), including tasks such as repairing roads, digging ditches, planting trees or working on quarries. Each worker was given a uniform, spade and a bicycle. Work was often far away from home so the men would live in barracks or camps.

It was unpopular as the work was hard, living and working conditions poor and the pay very low. However, those in the RAD were classed as employed so the scheme did help to reduce unemployment.

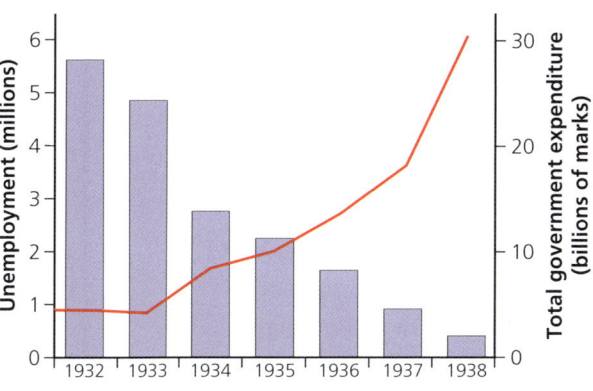

▲ Unemployment and government expenditure in Germany, 1932–38

▲ Hitler breaking ground for the autobahn between Frankfurt and Mannheim

Autobahns and public works schemes

Public works schemes were introduced to build new homes and improve transport by building bridges, new roads and canals. Building **autobahns** (motorways) was an important part of the public works schemes. The Nazis insisted that much of the work was done without heavy machinery in order to create more jobs.

On 23 September 1933, Hitler shovelled some soil in a ceremony near Stuttgart to kickstart Germany's autobahn programme. The government spent five billion Reichsmarks on this programme over a five year period. In 1934, 38,000 workers were employed on the autobahn scheme. In the end, 2000 miles of road was built. The autobahns were used as a propaganda success but only made a small impact in reducing unemployment.

Rearmament

In 1935, Hitler introduced conscription. This meant that all adult men between 18 and 25 had to do military service for two years. The army grew from 100,000 (its limit by the Treaty of Versailles) in 1933 to 1.4 million by 1939, creating more jobs.

Meanwhile, from 1936, the German economy helped prepare for war. New tanks, battleships and planes were ordered. Many factories got ready to support the military. The iron, steel and chemical industries grew and more oil, aluminium, rubber, explosives, steel and coal were produced.

Hitler's rearmament plans created lots of new employment opportunities in the army and in industries supplying the army. In fact, the plan cut down unemployment so much that it had created a labour shortage by 1939.

Invisible unemployment

In many ways, the Nazis played the statistics to make it seem that they had solved unemployment. In reality, there were more unemployed people than official statistics said. This was called 'invisible unemployment'.

> ### Exam Tip
>
> **Explaining why (Question 2)**
>
> Look at the advice on page 49 on how to tackle this type of question and produce a high-level explanation.
>
> Remember
>
> 1. **Decode** – What is the focus of this question?
> 2. **Decide** – How are you going to organise your answer?
> 3. **Develop** – Explain why the Nazis were able to reduce unemployment.

> ### Apply ▶ Exam Practice
>
> **Question 2 style**
>
> Explain why the Nazis were able to reduce unemployment in the years 1933 to 1939.
>
> **You may use the following in your answer:**
> - Invisible unemployment
> - Rearmament
>
> **You must also use information of your own.** (12 marks)

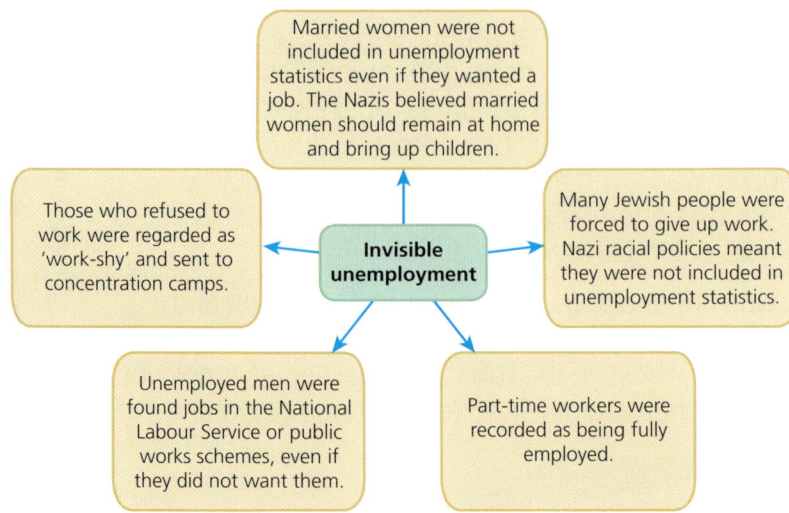

3.2 Changes in the standard of living

> **Research & Record**
>
> **Did the standard of living of German people improve?**
>
> Read pages 105–107. Gather evidence to support the views in the table. You will be able to use these notes to answer question 3d on page 108.
>
> | Interpretation | Support |
> |---|---|
> | The standard of living for German people improved in the 1930s. | |
> | The standard of living for German people did not improve in the 1930s. | |

Changes for German Workers

As the 1930s progressed, unemployment reduced and there were actually labour shortages by 1939. This meant there was more work available, which enabled more people to at least enjoy a regular wage. Other changes and policies meant that life for a range of workers changed as a result of Nazi economic policies.

Winter Aid

In September 1933, the Nazis created a scheme called 'Winter Aid' to support the poorest workers. Donations were supposed to be voluntary but in reality people were pressured to donate. The scheme gave out soup, food parcels and clothes to the poor. Although some of the poorest benefited from the handouts, Winter Aid donations could take up to 3 per cent of a worker's income and were in reality an extra burden for many.

Wages and working hours

Wages began to rise from 1933 and especially between 1936 and 1939. However, wages did not keep pace with price inflation. There was a big increase in food prices, meaning poorer workers were worse off than richer ones.

In 1933, the Nazis passed a law to increase taxes on big department stores to protect small businesses. However, small businesses could not compete with large ones. The emphasis on rearmament after 1935 meant big businesses such as IB Farben and Daimler-Benz expanded greatly at the expense of small businesses. Siemens dominated the electrical industry. Big businesses kept wages down and made people work harder, resulting in workers having to work longer hours for less pay. Working hours increased from an average of 43 hours per week in 1933 to 47 hours per week in 1939.

Farmers

Farmers saw their income increase by 41 per cent between 1933 and 1938. A law to protect small farms by making it harder to sell a farm to big business actually stifled modernisation of the farming industry. It was also harder to get farm workers, with many leaving the countryside for the city to work. Workers could earn more money in the armaments industry than on farms.

The German Labour Front (DAF)

Four days after trade unions were banned on 2 May 1933, the Nazis created the German Labour Front (DAF). It was headed by **Robert Ley**. This led to workers' rights being reduced, and workers could no longer go on strike. This was a key reason why most workers worked longer hours and in worse working conditions under Nazi rule.

Any worker who protested was deemed as 'work-shy' and could be sent to a concentration camp.

The German Labour Front created organisations to improve workers' lives. There was **Strength Through Joy**, **Beauty of Labour** and also a scheme to buy a **Volkswagen** car.

▶ **Source A** Memorandum circulating in the Reich Labour Ministry in 1936

Tourist trips, plays and concerts are not going to clear away any poverty-ridden slums or fill hungry mouths.

Strength Through Joy (KDF)

Strength Through Joy was created in November 1933. It organised the leisure time of German workers with various activities, as you can see in the mind map on the left. Strength Through Joy gave German workers leisure activities that normally would have only been enjoyed by the rich. By 1937, the Nazis were spending 29 million Reichsmarks on it. Over half of all theatre bookings in Berlin in 1938 were being made via Strength Through Joy.

Its biggest impact was on tourism. It enabled German workers to go on holiday. This was popular. By 1937, 1.7 million workers had enjoyed a Strength Through Joy package holiday. In 1939, 175,000 Germans travelled to Italy. Strength Through Joy cruises also served to indoctrinate people in Nazi ideas.

However, often the facilities for Strength Through Joy were poor. Accommodation on the holidays was sometimes in mass dormitories or had poor sanitation. Theatre tickets were often the worst tickets available, or theatres put on special performances for Strength Through Joy ticket-holders that were not as high quality. As Source A notes, the range of activities on offer did not always make up for the poverty that many Germans were living in.

▶ Workers travelling on a 'Strength Through Joy' excursion, 1935. The sign reads 'Strength Through Joy'

Beauty of Labour

Beauty of Labour was a department of Strength Through Joy. The idea was that it would compensate for the longer working hours. It arranged the following:

Beauty of Labour initiatives
- Better washing facilities, showers and toilets
- New changing rooms and lockers
- Hygiene and cleanliness campaigns
- Better ventilation in the workplace
- Less noise in the factory
- Cleaning up waste in the workplace

▼ **Source B** A 1938 advert for the Volkswagen produced by the German Labour Front, with the idealised Aryan German family

The Nazis believed if workers had better conditions then they would work harder. However, many of these improvements were expected to be done by the workers themselves, after hours with no extra pay. If workers did not take part, they could be threatened with the sack or even being sent to a concentration camp.

Volkswagen scheme

The German Labour Front created a scheme in 1938 for workers to pay into a weekly scheme where they could buy a Volkswagen (People's Car). By the end of 1939, 340,000 German workers had invested into the scheme. There was much propaganda around it. However, in the end, hardly any German workers who paid into the scheme got a Volkswagen car. This was because Volkswagen went into military production as Germany focused on rearmament.

Apply ▶ Recall Challenge

Source B shows you an example of Nazi propaganda.
1. Mind map five ways in which the Nazis used propaganda to keep control of people in Nazi Germany.
2. Choose one of the following events from Part 3 of the Weimar and Nazi Germany course. Mind map everything you can remember about it.

- Reichstag Fire
- Night of the Long Knives
- The Berlin Olympics
- The Concordat
- The story of Martin Niemöller

Revision Tip

Regularly connect and retrieve information.
1. Making connections between new learning and prior learning will help you remember key information. Here, you can connect the Volkswagen poster with other examples of Nazi propaganda.
2. Regularly retrieve information from other parts of the course. Spacing out your revision helps you remember it well.

Apply — Exam Practice

Question 3b style

Study Interpretations 1 and 2.

They give different views about whether the Nazis improved people's standard of living. What is the main difference between these views?

Explain your answer, using details from *both* interpretations. (4 marks)

Question 3c style

Suggest **one** reason why Interpretations 1 and 2 give different views about whether the Nazis improved people's standard of living.

You may use Sources A and B to help explain your answer. (4 marks)

Question 3d style

How far do you agree with Interpretation 2 about whether the Nazis improved people's standard of living?

Explain your answer, using *both* interpretations and your knowledge of the historical context. (16 marks)

▶ **Interpretation 1** Geoff Layton in *Democracy and Nazism: Germany 1918–1945*, 2019

There was a dramatic growth in jobs. From the registered peak of 6 million unemployed in January 1932, the official figure for 1936 showed it had declined to 2.1 million. For those many Germans who had been desperately out of work, the Nazi economic policy was to be welcomed. Even in other democratic countries scarred by mass unemployment, observers abroad admired Germany's achievement of job creation.

▶ **Interpretation 2** Richard J. Evans, *The Third Reich in Power*, 2005

Even on the prestigious motorway projects, working conditions were so poor, food rations so low and hours so long that there were frequent protests, all the way to the burning down of the workers' barracks. Many of those drafted onto the projects, such as hairdressers, white-collar workers or travelling salesmen, were wholly unsuited to hard physical labour. Accidents were frequent and repeated. Complainers were sent to Dachau. Such measures also helped, along with strict labour controls and the abolition of unions, to keep net real wages down.

Exam Tip

Support your answer with specific knowledge (Question 3d)

In the exam, you can improve your explanations by including relevant facts to support your arguments. For example, when answering this question:

- Do not simply say that 'the Nazis did not improve people's standard of living'.
- Say 'The Nazis did not improve people's standard of living **because** the working week rose from 43 hours to 47 hours. This shows that despite people having jobs they were working longer hours and often for less money.'

Exam Tip

Analysing an interpretation (Question 3d)

Look again at the advice at how to approach this type of question on pages 28, 56 and 88.

To analyse the view in Interpretation 2, you could select a quote that shows the view of the historian and then use your own knowledge to agree, and later Interpretation 1 to disagree, with this quotation and view.

For example, the author of interpretation 2 argues that the Nazis did not improve people's standard of living as 'working conditions were so poor'. We can use Interpretation 1 to disagree with this view as it argues that unemployment had declined from 6 million in 1932 to 2.1 million by 1926 and was 'admired' by 'other democratic countries'. Our own knowledge of the Beauty of Labour department can also be used to disagree and show that the Nazis did what they could to improve the conditions for workers.

4 The persecution of minorities

4.1 Nazi racial beliefs and policies and treatment of minority groups

> **Research & Record**
>
> **Who did the Nazis persecute and why?**
> Read the information on this page, then:
> 1 Explain what the Nazi racial beliefs were. Make sure you understand the key words of **Herrenvolk** and **Untermenschen**.
> 2 Make notes about each of the groups the Nazis persecuted and the reasons why. For each group, record when, how and why they were persecuted.

Nazi racial beliefs

The Nazis incorrectly believed that all humans can be scientifically grouped into different races and that there is a racial hierarchy. They believed in what they called the **Aryan** race – tall and athletic, with blonde hair and blue eyes, which was superior to all other races: the **Herrenvolk** (master race).

The Nazis thought that all other races were **Untermenschen** (subhumans). Rather than being a religious group, Hitler wrongly believed that there was such a thing as a Jewish race. For the Nazis, Jewish people were the lowest of all human races. The Nazis defined someone as being Jewish if they had three or four Jewish grandparents.

Nazi racial policies

Nazi views on race led them to treat different people in different ways. Some groups were persecuted because of how the Nazis viewed their 'race'.

The Nazis believed in **eugenics**, a pseudo-science that believes human populations can be 'improved' through 'selective breeding'. They only wanted who they regarded as the 'best' Germans – perfect Aryans – to have children. Those people who they did not regard as 'perfect' were persecuted – they were treated badly by the Nazis because of things like their disability, their sexuality or their race. Those considered 'unsuitable' were sterilised to prevent them from having children.

> **Connect & Engage**
>
> **Nazi racial beliefs**
>
> Study Source A on page 110 and connect it with your learning.
> 1 What have you already learned about Hitler's attitude towards what he believed were non-Aryan races such as Jewish people?
> 2 What can you infer from Source A about Nazi attitudes to Jewish people?

▲ **Source A** The source shows a teacher teaching a class Nazi views about Jewish people.

Slavs

Slavs were people who had migrated into Europe from the east hundreds of years ago. Their modern descendants can be found in Eastern Europe and many were living in Germany in the 1930s. Although they were not targeted as much as other groups, the Nazis taught that Slavs were Untermenschen. Slav countries in Eastern Europe, such as Poland, were seen as inferior to other countries. The Nazis threatened to invade these countries in order to gain 'living space' for Aryans. This would happen in the Second World War.

Roma and Sinti people

The Nazis singled out Roma and Sinti people for **persecution** because they were not Aryans. They also disapproved of their travelling lifestyle and believed they were criminals because they did not do ordinary work. Many Roma and Sinti people were sent to concentration camps in 1933. In 1938, Roma and Sinti people were banned from travelling in groups. In 1939, orders were made to deport all Roma and Sinti people out of Germany. During the Second World War, the Romani Holocaust saw between 250,000 and 500,000 Roma and Sinti people murdered by the Nazis.

People with disabilities

People with disabilities, including those with physical and mental illnesses, were also targeted by the Nazis. Three hundred and fifty thousand men and women with inherited conditions were sterilised without their consent. The Nazis began to put these people to death. The policy was known as euthanasia. In 1939, 5200 children with disabilities were murdered by the Nazis.

LGBTQ+ people

As in most other parts of Europe, same-sex relationships in Germany had been illegal for many years. The Weimar Republic was more tolerant than previous governments and attempts were made to change the law. The Nazis believed that homosexuality weakened Germany. Gay and bisexual men were persecuted terribly. Around 15,000 were arrested and imprisoned after trial for breaking the law. When released, however, many were sent to concentration camps. There they were very harshly treated. Some were sterilised or used in medical experiments to try to force them to be attracted to women.

Connect & Engage – Victor Klemperer (1881–1960)

Victor Klemperer was a German Jew, born in 1881. He was an academic, journalist and writer. During the First World War, he fought in the German army and received a medal for bravery.

Professor Klemperer

After the war, he became a professor at Dresden Technical University. Klemperer and his wife Eva had a comfortable life. They loved going to the cinema and enjoyed long cruises, including one trip to South America.

Dismissal and discrimination

Klemperer's life changed when the Nazis came to power in 1933. Hitler was fiercely **antisemitic** (against Jewish people). Klemperer waited with fear to see what would happen. Almost immediately, the Nazis began a campaign of **persecution**. Klemperer was dismissed from his job in 1935. Like other Jewish people in Germany, he was banned from owning a car, telephone, typewriter or radio. He could no longer enter a park or own a pet. He could not go to the cinema, library or swimming pool.

Persecution

In November 1938, on a night that became known as '**Kristallnacht**', 91 Jewish people were killed and 30,000 more arrested. This was the point at which Klemperer realised that there was no one and nothing to protect Jewish people.

In May 1940, the Klemperers were forced to move into a 'Jewish people' house. Jewish people were made to wear a yellow star. Nowhere felt safe.

Survival

By February 1945, Klemperer, now aged 63, was one of only 198 Jewish people left in the city and district of Dresden. On Tuesday 13 February, he was ordered to report for deportation. However, after Dresden was bombed by the Allies, the Klemperers escaped. They blended in with the other German people leaving the city.

The Klemperers went on the run across Germany for the next three months. They ended up in a village in southern Germany. Victor survived the Second World War, and the diaries he kept while living under Nazi rule were published in 1995.

Connect & Engage

Read Victor Klemperer's story.
1. What do you remember most about his story?
2. How did his life change as a result of Nazi rule?
3. What do you find the most shocking about this story?

4.2 The persecution of Jewish people

Research & Record

How did Nazi policies change the lives of Jewish people living in Germany?

Study the information on these three pages.

1. Create five category cards like this to sum up Nazi measures against Jewish people. Make one card for each of these categories:
   - Work
   - Leisure
   - Education
   - Citizenship
   - Safety
2. Think carefully about the **consequences** of the measure you have placed in each category. Produce a **consequences** card for each category.

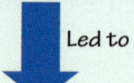

CATEGORY CARD
WORK – Jewish businesses were boycotted and attacked. Jewish people were banned from many different jobs.

Led to

CONSEQUENCE CARD
Jewish people struggled to make enough money to survive. Many lived in poverty and struggled to buy food and clothes. Jewish people also felt shut out of society.

Jewish people before 1933

In 1933, Jewish people made up 1 per cent of the German population and were well integrated into German society. Marriages between Jewish people and people of other faiths were quite common. Although some Jewish people were wealthy and owned businesses, many did not and Jewish people came from all classes in society.

Hitler claimed that Jewish people caused Germany to lose the First World War. This is not true. Many German Jewish people fought bravely in the First World War with some receiving medals for bravery.

When Hitler came to power in January 1933, the lives of all German Jewish people changed for the worse.

Boycott of Jewish shops and businesses

In April 1933, the Nazis organised an official **boycott** of Jewish shops and businesses so other German people did not shop in them. Members of the SA stood outside Jewish shops and places of business. The Star of David was painted on many shop doors and signs were painted saying 'Don't buy from Jews'. Throughout Germany there were acts of violence against Jewish people and Jewish businesses. The police rarely acted to protect Jewish people. Although many Germans ignored the boycott, the event began the organised persecution of Jewish people.

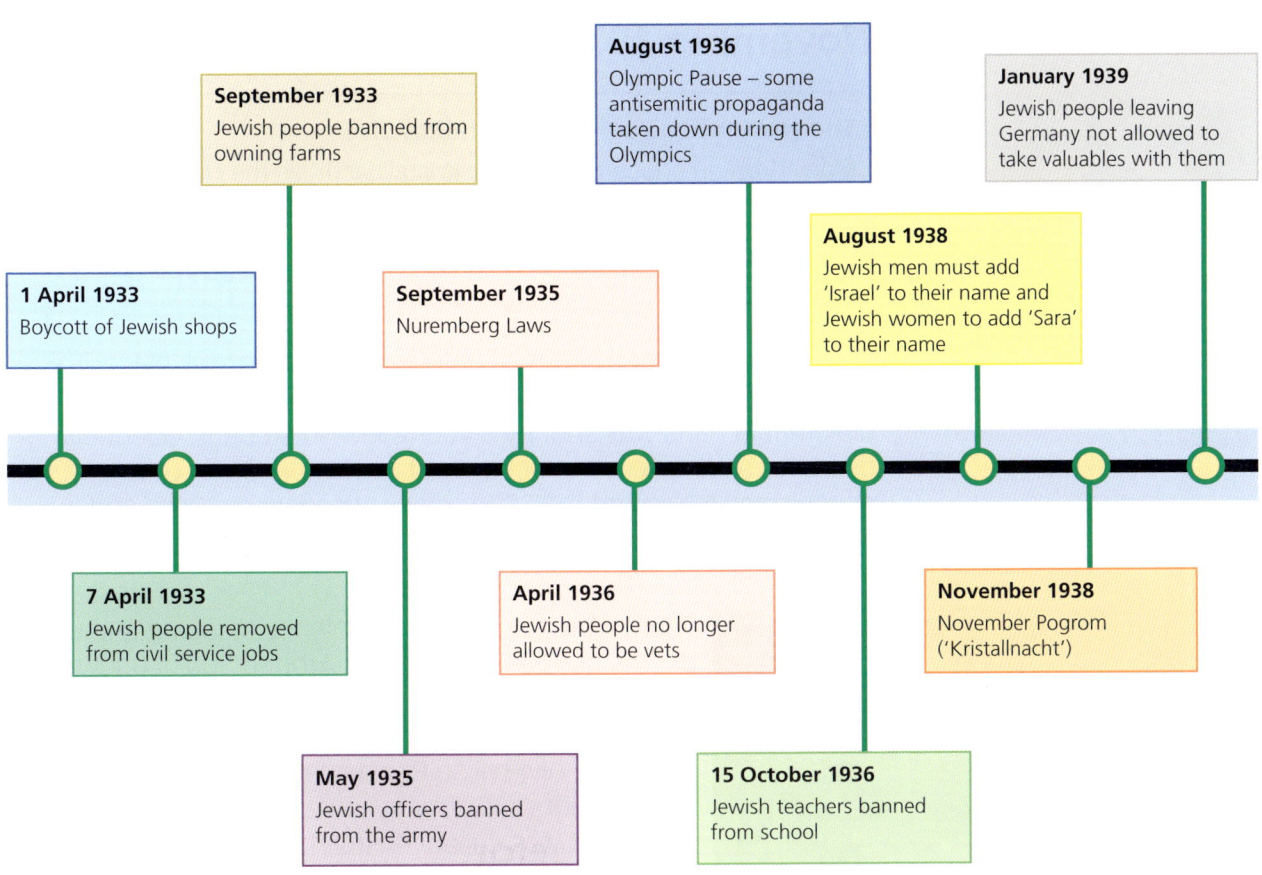

▲ Some of the antisemitic laws and actions taken against Jewish people in Nazi Germany

1935: The Nuremberg Laws

Discrimination got worse in 1935. Hitler announced the **Nuremberg Laws** at the September 1935 Nuremberg Rally. The Nuremberg Laws were a turning point because they showed that discrimination against Jewish people was going to get worse.

> ### Nuremberg Laws
>
> **Law for the Protection of German Blood and German Honour** – this made marriage and sexual relations between Jewish people and Aryans illegal.
>
> **Reich Citizenship Law** – this meant German Jews were no longer citizens of Germany. German Jews were now 'subjects' and had no legal rights. They could no longer vote in elections.
>
>
>
> ◀ A sign saying 'Jews are not wanted at the Baltic Sea Resort of Rauschen!'

> ▶ **Source B** Victor Klemperer remembers the Olympic Pause
>
> People at home and abroad are constantly being told that they are here witnessing the revival, the blossoming, the new mind, the unity, the steadfastness and glory, of course also the peacefulness of the spirit of the Third Reich, that lovingly embraces the entire world. The slogan-chanting mobs are banned (for the duration of the Olympics), campaigns against the Jews, warlike speeches, everything disreputable has vanished from the newspapers until 16 August, and still, day and night, the swastika flags are flying everywhere.

November 1938: 'Kristallnacht'

> **The November Pogrom ('Kristallnacht')**
> Many German educators refer to 'Kristallnacht' as the November Pogrom. This is because the word 'Kristallnacht' came from ordinary Germans and is an example of perpetrator language. They don't believe the word fully describes the extreme violence that actually took place.

On 9–10 November a series of anti-Jewish attacks took place. This is an example of a **pogrom**. The event was sparked when a German diplomat in Paris was shot by a young Jewish student. Goebbels used this as an excuse to act against Jewish people in Germany. He encouraged Nazis and the SS to attack synagogues, German Jews and their homes and businesses. The police were given orders not to stop them.

▲ Germans pass by the smashed windows of a Jewish-owned shop; the aftermath of 'Kristallnacht' (Night of Broken Glass), 9–10 November 1938

There were two nights of violence resulting in the deaths of 91 Jewish people. Around 300,000 Jewish men were sent to concentration camps. The Jewish people were blamed for the violence and ordered to pay a fine of 1 billion Reichsmarks for the damage. As many streets in Germany were left with broken glass, the attack was called 'Kristallnacht' (the Night of the Broken Glass) by many ordinary German people.

Although violence against Jews had increased, this was the first organised violence against the Jewish people. The event was a turning point in the treatment of Jews as many ordinary German people became bystanders and did not protest. Many German Jewish people realised that they were no longer safe and hundreds of thousands tried to find ways to leave Germany.

1939 – Further erosion of rights and liberties

Many German Jewish people continued trying to emigrate in 1939. Jewish emigrants were not allowed to take valuables with them when they left the country. By September 1939, there was a curfew and Jewish people could no longer leave their homes after 8 p.m.

In September 1939, the Second World War broke out and this would lead to the Nazi plans for the 'Final Solution', which would result in the murder of 6 million Jewish people. The events of 1933 to 1939 had prepared Germany for one of the most horrific genocides (killing of a race of people) in history.

Between 1933 and 1939, 282,000 Jewish people managed to emigrate from Germany and start new lives abroad. Tragically, many moved to neighbouring countries which would be taken over by Germany during the Second World War.

Part 4: Review

Apply ▶ Recall Challenge

Key individuals

Study these individuals.

- Baldur von Schirach
- Trude Mohr
- Victor Klemperer

For each one, try to answer these questions from memory. Get somebody else to test you.
- Who were they?
- What was their impact and importance?

Key organisations and groups

Study these key organisations.

- Hitler Youth
- League of German Maidens
- Strength Through Joy
- Beauty of Labour
- German Labour Front

For each organisation fill in this table to help you recall the details.

What?	When?	Who?	What happened?

Know your key words

Read the following key words and write a definition of each one. Use the glossary to help you remember some of the main words if you get stuck. Get somebody else to test you on the meaning of the key words.

Life in Hitler's Germany, 1933–39			
Race studies	Eugenics	Indoctrination	Invisible unemployment
Autobahns	National Labour Service	German Labour Front (DAF)	Slavs
Roma and Sinti	Untermenschen	Aryan	Master Race (Herrenvolk)
Antisemitism	'Kristallnacht'	Nuremberg Laws	Boycott

Exam Tip

Explaining why (Question 2)

Use the 3Ds to tackle this exam question and produce a high-level explanation.

Remember the 3Ds:

Decode – What is the focus of this question?

Decide – How are you going to organise your answer?

Develop – Explain why. Use the connectives below to help you.

This led to …
This resulted in …
This meant that …

Apply ▶ Exam Practice

Question 2 style

Explain how persecution towards Jewish people in Nazi Germany increased in the years 1933 to 1939.

You may use the following in your answer:
- The boycott of Jewish shops (1933)
- The Nuremberg Laws (1935)

You must also use information of your own.

(12 marks)

Review the whole course

Task 1 Answer the big questions

Look at the key content in the introduction to the course (pages 6–7). Choose one of the topics and make a revision mind-map from memory to recall your knowledge.

Task 2 Create flashcards

On pages 117–118 there is a glossary of key words, events and individuals. Use this to create a set of revision flashcards that can help you revise each of the key words, events and individuals you have covered on this course.

- On the front of the card, write some questions that can help test your knowledge of the word/event/individual when you next revise the topic. For example, if you were making a flashcard on the Kapp Putsch, you could write down these questions.
- On the back of the card, record the definition of the key word or details about the word, event or individual.

> **Kapp Putsch**
> - Who was involved?
> - What were their aims?
> - When did it happen?
> - Where did it happen?
> - What happened?
> - Why was it important?

Revision Tips

Use flashcards to test knowledge and understanding

1. Once you have completed your flashcards, use them regularly to test yourself.
   a. Try to answer the questions on the front of the card without looking anything up.
   b. Sort the cards into three piles: red, amber and green, according to how confident you are.
   - **Green**: I have a very good understanding
   - **Amber**: I have a good understanding but forgot a few points. You should return to these cards again within a week.
   - **Red**: I struggled with this. Return to these cards as often as you can until you are confident enough to put them in the amber pile.

Use flashcards to practise answering exam questions

2. Choose a 12-mark exam question from this book or from a past exam paper. Then select the flashcards that will help you answer the question. To help plan your answer, put the cards into the order to answer the question and write a paragraph on each card.

Key words, individuals and events

> **Revision Tip**
>
> Check your understanding of key words, individuals and events using this glossary. Use the following revision tips to help you recall them.
>
> 1. Make flashcards. Write the name on one side of a card and the definition on the other side and practise testing yourself.
> 2. Ask somebody else to test you on the meaning of the key word.
> 3. Write out the key word and create a mind map by linking relevant key information to it.
> 4. Organise the information into the following categories and then complete the tasks:
>   - **Individuals** – write down five ways in which this person was significant
>   - **Key group** – write down five ways in which the key group was significant
>   - **Key events** – write down five things you can recall about the event. You could focus on causes or consequences.

Abdicate When a monarch gives up being king or queen.

Armistice An agreement to stop fighting.

Aryan The Nazi term for the German 'race'. Nazis believed in a northern European, Aryan racial group that was pure and superior to all other races.

Bamberg Conference A Nazi meeting of 1926 where Hitler gained more control of the Nazi Party.

Bauhaus A popular style of art, design and architecture in 1920s Germany.

Beauty of Labour An organisation in Nazi Germany for improving working conditions.

Boycott Refusing to buy goods and services as a form of protest. The Nazis organised a boycott of Jewish shops in April 1933.

Chancellor The leader of Germany – a similar role to the Prime Minister of the UK.

Communism A political ideology of a society where everyone is equal and there is no private property.

Concordat An agreement made between the Nazis and the Catholic Church in July 1933.

Constitution A system of rules which sets out how a country will be run.

Culture The customs, beliefs and ideas of a society.

Dawes Plan An economic plan made in August 1924 to help Germany pay its reparations.

Edelweiss Pirates A mainly working-class youth group who rebelled against Nazi ideas.

Enabling Act A law passed in March 1933 which gave Hitler the power to make laws himself.

Freikorps An organisation of former soldiers who had fought in the First World War.

Führer German word for leader. This was the title Hitler had after the death of President von Hindenburg in August 1934.

German Revolution This took place at the end of the First World War. It saw the abdication of Kaiser Wilhelm II and the creation of a new democratic system of government called the Weimar Republic.

German Labour Front (DAF) An organisation set up by the Nazis to represent workers after Trade Unions were abolished.

Gestapo The German Secret Police.

Hyperinflation When the price of goods increases very rapidly because the value of money falls.

Kapp Putsch An armed uprising in 1920 against the government, led by Wolfgang Kapp and the Freikorps.

'Kristallnacht' Night of the Broken Glass. This took place in November 1938 and was when Jewish people, property and synagogues were attacked throughout Germany.

League of German Maidens Nazi Youth Organisation for girls.

League of Nations International organisation set up after the First World War to promote peace and settle disputes. Germany joined in 1926.

Mein Kampf 'My Struggle'. This was the book that Hitler wrote while in prison in 1924 which set out Hitler's ideas and plans for Germany.

Munich Putsch Armed Nazi uprising that took place in November 1923. Its failure led to Hitler and other Nazis being sent to prison.

Nazi Party The National Socialist German Worker's Party (NSDAP or 'Nazi' for short) was the political party of Adolf Hitler.

Niemöller, Martin An important German Protestant pastor (priest) who became a vocal opponent of the Nazis.

Night of the Long Knives Event of June 1934 when SA leaders including Ernst Röhm were arrested and murdered.

Nuremberg Laws Laws introduced by the Nazis in 1935 to strip Jewish people of German citizenship and civil rights.

Persecution Ill treatment of a person or group usually due to their ethnicity, religion, gender or sexual orientation.

Propaganda spreading politically biased messages to gain support for a political group or leader – e.g. through newspapers, rallies, posters, radio and film.

Reich Church Group of Protestant Churches who united under a new Nazi-influenced Protestant Church overseen by Ludwig Müller.

Reichstag The German Parliament.

Reichstag Fire The burning down of the German Parliament in February 1933. The Nazis blamed it on a Dutch Communist called Marinus van der Lubbe and said it was the start of a communist revolution.

Reparations Payments to be made by Germany to the Allies due to the damage done during the First World War. The amount was fixed in 1921 but in reality Germany paid very little of the reparations.

Röhm, Ernst A leading Nazi and leader of the SA. Röhm was killed during the Night of the Long Knives in June 1934.

Ruhr An industrial area in Germany.

SA Sturmabteilung (Stormtroopers). Known as the Brownshirts, the SA were set up by Hitler to protect his meetings and intimidate political opponents.

SS Schutzstaffel (Protection Squad). Know as the Blackshirts, the SS began as Hitler's private bodyguard. They were responsible for Nazi terror between 1933 and 1939.

Spartacist Rising An attempt by the German Communists to take power in January 1919.

Stab in the Back Myth Dolchstosslegende. The belief that Germany had not been properly defeated in the First World War but had been betrayed by politicians of the Weimar Republic.

Strength Through Joy Nazi organisation focused on providing leisure activities and entertainment to German workers.

Stresemann, Gustav An important politician in the 1920s who helped stabilise Germany. He was Chancellor in 1923 and then Foreign Minister from 1924 until his death in 1929.

Swing Youth A group of young people in Germany who did not support the Nazis. Instead, they embraced foreign music, fashion and lifestyle.

Treaty of Versailles A peace treaty signed on 28 June 1919 between Germany and the Allies. It was widely hated in Germany and seen as humiliating due to loss of land, resources and military restrictions.

von Hindenburg, Paul Former First World War military leader and President of Germany between 1925 and 1934.

von Papen, Franz A German politician and Chancellor who helped Hitler rise to power.

Wall Street Crash A sudden fall in stock prices on the US stock exchange in Wall Street, New York in 1929. This led to the Great Depression, which had a devastating effect on Germany, resulting in 6 million being unemployed.

Weimar Republic the name of the German government from 1918 to 1933. The name originated from the fact the government was initially based in a town in central Germany called Weimar.

Weltpolitik World politics

Wilhelm II (Kaiser) German emperor/king/monarch. He ruled from 1888 until his abdication in November 1918.

Young Plan An agreement made between Germany and the Allies to further lower reparations, allowing Germany to pay them over a longer time.

INDEX

A
abortion 33, 94
Allies 11, 13, 16, 19
architecture 35, 79
7, 69
armies, unofficial 19, 40, 47, 55
armistice 12, 13
art 34, 78
Aryan race 109
assassinations 19
autobahns 104
autocracy 10

B
Bamberg Conference 47
Bauhaus 35
Beauty of Labour 7, 107
Berlin Olympics (1936) 74, 76
Bolshevik Revolution 11
book burning 30, 78, 79
Brownshirts 40, 64
  see also Sturmabteilung (SA)

C
cabaret 33, 35
Catholicism 81, 86
censorship 6, 75
Christianity 80, 86
Church
  control of 80–2
  opposition from 6, 84, 86
cinema 35
communism 13, 17, 18, 52, 54, 66
concentration camps 72, 106, 107
Concordat 81–2
conscription 104
constitution 14–15, 27, 31, 33, 66
courts 72–3
crime 51
culture
  Nazi control of 74–9
  Weimar Republic 30, 33–5
currency 22, 25
  see also hyperinflation

D
Dawes Plan 24–5
democracy 12, 15, 51, 64
dictatorship 66–7, 69–73
disabilities, people with 110
Drexler, Anton 39

E
Ebert, Friedrich 12, 18–19, 27
economy
  crisis 6, 13, 20–3
  currency 22
  hyperinflation 20–3
  inflation 13, 20
  recovery 6, 24–5
  see also Great Depression
Edelweiss Pirates 87
education 101
employment 7, 32, 103–7
Enabling Act (1933) 6, 66, 72
eugenics 109

F
farming 51, 54, 105
film industry 74, 79
First World War 10–12, 17, 38
flu epidemic 13
food shortages 13
Freikorps. 13, 18–19
Freisier, Roland 73

G
gender 30
  see also LGBTQ+ people
German Communist Party (KPD) 18, 52
German Faith Movement 81
German Labour Front (DAF) 66, 106
German National Party (DNVP) 19, 27
German Revolution 12
German Workers' Party (DAP) 38–9
Gestapo 71–2
Goebbels, Joseph 6, 47, 55, 66, 68, 74–5, 114
Goering, Hermann 40, 71
Great Depression 15, 31, 50, 55
Gropius, Walter 35

H
Hauer, Joseph 81
Hess, Rudolf 40
Himmler, Heinrich 6, 71, 94
Hirschfeld, Magnus 30, 78
Hitler, Adolf 6
  assasination attempts 83
  as Chancellor 58–60, 64
  dictatorship 6, 66–7, 69–73
  early years 38
  as Führer 40, 55–6, 69
  Mein Kampf 44, 46, 79
  prison 44, 46
  rise to power 6, 39–44, 47, 54–6
Hitler Youth 47, 99–100
housing 31
hyperinflation 6, 20–3

I
inflation 13, 20

J
Jehovah's Witnesses 86
Jewish people 18, 49, 55, 109, 112–14

K
Kaiser Wilhelm II 6, 10, 12
Kapp, Wolfgang 19, 42
Kapp Putsch 19, 42
Kellogg-Briand Pact 24
Kiel, mutiny of sailors 12, 13
Klemperer, Victor 111, 113
Kristallnacht 7, 111, 114

L
League of German Maidens 97, 100
League of Nations 26
legal system 72–3
leisure 106
  see also culture
LGBTQ+ people 30, 110
Liebknecht, Karl 18
literature 35, 79
living standards 7, 31, 105
Locarno Pact 24, 26
Ludendorff, Erich 42
Luxemburg, Rosa 6, 18

M
marriage 93
Marxism 18
Mein Kampf 44, 46, 79
mental illness 110
minority groups 7, 109
Mohr, Trude 97
Munich Putsch 6, 42–5
murders, political 19, 67
music 35, 79

N
nationalism 55
National Labour Service 103
National Socialist German Workers' Party (NSDAP) 38–9, 41
  Twenty-Five Point Programme 39
Nazi Party
  election success 59–60
  opposition to 6, 48–9, 64, 83–8
  rise of 6, 15, 19, 39–40, 47, 50, 53–6
Neue Sachlichkeit 34
newspapers 77
Niemöller, Martin 6, 82, 84, 86
nightclubs 33, 35
Night of the Long Knives 6, 47, 63, 67
November Criminals 12, 55
Nuremberg Laws 113
Nuremberg rallies 76

O
Olympics (1936) 74, 76
Owens, Jesse 76

P
Parliament see Reichstag
passive resistance 20
peace treaty see Treaty of Versailles
pogroms 114
police state 71–2
political murders 19
political parties, Weimar Republic 14, 19, 27, 66
poverty 51, 106
Preuss, Hugo 15
propaganda 6, 11, 12, 39, 52, 55, 66, 74–6, 94
proportional representation 15

R
racial policies 109
radio 77
rallies 76
rearmament 104
Reich Church 82
Reichstag 10, 14, 32, 52–3, 59–60, 66, 68
Reichstag Fire 6, 65–6
Rentenmark 22, 25
reparations 17, 20, 22, 25
Riefenstahl, Leni 74
Röhm, Ernst 40, 47, 55, 63–4, 67

Index

Roma communities 110
Ruhr, occupation of 20, 22
Russia 11

S

Schacht, Hjalmar 22
Scientific Humanitarian Committee 30
sexuality 30, 33
Sieg Heil salute 40, 73
Sinti communities 110
Slavs 110
Spanish flu 13
Spartacist Rising 6, 18–19, 52
Speer, Albert 79
sport 76
SS (Schutzstaffel) 47, 71
Stab in the Back Myth 12, 16, 38, 55
Stalhelm (Steel Helmets) 19
sterilisation, forced 110
Stinnes, Hugo 21
Streicher, Julius 40
Strength Through Joy 7, 106
Stresemann, Gustav 6, 22, 24–6, 28, 48
strikes 13, 19, 52
Sturmabteilung (SA) 19, 40, 47, 55, 64
swastika 40, 73
Swing Youth 87

T

taxation 31
Thälmann, Ernst 52
theatre 35, 106
trade unions 32, 52, 66, 106
Treaty of Versailles 6, 16–17, 19, 24–6, 54

U

unemployment 7, 15, 25, 31, 50–3, 95, 104

V

Volksgemeinschaft 55
Volkswagen scheme 107
von Hindenburg, Paul 6, 27, 48, 59–60, 64, 66, 67, 69
von Papen, Franz 6, 57, 59–60, 64, 67
von Schirach, Baldur 97
von Schleicher, Kurt 59–60
voting rights 15, 32

W

Wall Street Crash (1929) 6, 50
war and conflict
  First World War 10–12, 17, 38
  occupation of the Ruhr 20, 22
  Second World War 114
Weimar Republic 6, 12
  challenges 16–22, 42, 51
  constitution 14–15, 27, 31, 33, 66
  Golden Years 24–35
  origins 13–14
  political parties 14, 19, 27, 66
welfare benefits 31
Weltpolitik 10, 24
Western Front 11, 12
Wilson, Woodrow 16
women
  Nazi policies 7, 47, 91–6
  rights of 32–3
  social freedom 33, 95
  voting rights 15, 32
  in Weimar Republic 32
  and work 32, 95
working conditions 31, 107

Y

young people 7, 47, 87, 97–102
Young Plan 24–5, 27